C000071898

The
Economist
Books

POCKET

ACCOUNTING

CHRISTOPHER NOBES

THE ECONOMIST IN ASSOCIATION WITH
PROFILE BOOKS LTD

Profile Books Ltd
58A Hatton Garden, London EC1N 8LX

This edition published by Profile Books Ltd
in association with
The Economist 1998

Typeset in Garamond by MacGuru
macguru@pavilion.co.uk

Printed in Italy by
LEGO S.p.a. – Vicenza – Italy

A CIP catalogue record for this book is available
from the British Library

ISBN 1 86197 080 3

CONTENTS

Preface   iv
Understanding the basics   v

Part 1   Essays   **1**
Standard-setting in the 1990s   3
Accounting for goodwill and brands   9
International differences in accounting   13
Towards greater harmony   20

Part 2   A–Z   **27**
Alphabetical entries   29

Part 3   Appendixes   **177**

1 Abbreviations   177
2 World's largest accountancy firms   181
3 UK accounting standards   182
4 Useful addresses   183
5 Recommended reading   185

PREFACE

Accounting is an ancient art that played a key role in the development of writing and numbers. As commerce and government have become more complicated, accounting has kept pace with them, oiling the wheels of economic progress. The first known book with a substantial treatise on double entry was published in 1494 in Venice. One of Goethe's characters called double entry "one of the fairest inventions of the human mind": it usually appeals to those who like algebra, cryptic crosswords or Bach cello suites.

Thus accounting is no confused parvenu like economics. However, neither is it a science: there remains much judgment in accounting and, consequently, much controversy. This book is intended to be a guide to the jargon, the concepts and the uncertainties of accounting. Its basic context is the UK, but there are frequent references to and entries concerning the United States. In the case of many entries, knowledge of other entries is relevant; these are denoted by words in SMALL CAPITALS that indicate a cross-reference. There is also a list of abbreviations in Appendix 1. The world of accounting is changing fast, and the currency of this book will be affected by changes in 1998 and subsequent years.

My thanks are due to my colleague, Bob Parker, for hundreds of helpful comments; and to Carol Wright for the use of great word-processing skill. I gratefully acknowledge the permission of Simon James and Bob Parker to cull their *Dictionary of Business Quotations* (Routledge, 1990) for the quotations sprinkled throughout my text. Naturally, errors and omissions in this book should appear as debits on my own account (in the reader's books).

Christopher Nobes

UNDERSTANDING THE BASICS

Those unfamiliar with accounting may like to begin by reading the following basic entries.

ACCOUNTANCY PROFESSION
ACCOUNTING PRINCIPLES
ACCOUNTING STANDARDS
ACCOUNTS
ASSETS
AUDITING
BALANCE SHEET
COMPANY
CONSOLIDATED FINANCIAL STATEMENTS
DEPRECIATION
HISTORICAL COST ACCOUNTING
LIABILITIES
MATCHING
MATERIALITY
PROFIT AND LOSS ACCOUNT
PRUDENCE
TRUE AND FAIR VIEW

"I would send her . . . to a boarding-school, in order to learn a little ingenuity and artifice. Then, Sir, she should have a supercilious knowledge of accounts; and as she grew up, I would have her instructed in geometry, that she might know something of the contagious countries."

Mrs Malaprop's views on education,
including that in accounting.
R.B. Sheridan, *The Rivals*, Act I, Scene II

Part 1
ESSAYS

STANDARD-SETTING IN THE 1990s

The Accounting Standards Board (ASB) took over standard-setting in the UK on August 1st 1990 from the Accounting Standards Committee (ASC), a committee of the accountancy profession. The ASC had been created in 1969 amid considerable turmoil when the profession feared that the government would intervene in accounting rule-making because of a series of accounting scandals and catastrophes and the resultant press criticism. By the end of the 1980s the ASC was itself criticised for weakness in the face of pressure from companies. The new UK standard-setting arrangements are summarised in Figure 1. The important point is that the ASB is not a committee of the accountancy profession and standards now have a legal status.

Figure 1 **Summary of UK standard-setting arrangements from 1990**

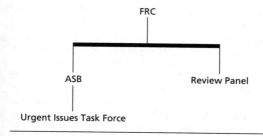

International comparisons

Comparisons between nine major countries will help to put these changes into context. It is useful to separate the creation of rules from their enforcement. In the case of both activities, an obvious two-group classification of players is into government and non-government. Traditionally, in the English-speaking world and the Netherlands, the creation and enforcement of accounting rules have been in the hands of the profession. Initially the rules were not written down, as in the UK up to the 1940s. Subsequently they became advisory for auditors, as in the UK up to 1970 and in the Netherlands now, then compulsory for auditors because of professional rules, as in the UK from 1970 and in some other major English-speaking countries now. Eventually the rules (now generally called "standards") may become compulsory for companies, as they are for US companies registered with the Securities and Exchange Commission (SEC), and in Canada and Australia because of company law. The UK moved towards this final position with the 1989 Companies Act.

The common feature of all these arrangements is that standards are not set by the government. This statement, however, is slightly misleading because the Department of Trade and Industry (DTI) in the UK and the SEC in the United States stand closely by the rule-makers. Clearly the standard-setters will make different rules if they know these can be enforced; hence the enormously more detailed and strict rules in the US compared with the UK.

A further subtlety is that these Anglo-Saxon non-governmental rule-makers are not necessarily from the accountancy profession. In Canada and New Zealand they are, but in the US this ceased to be the case with the formation of the Financial Accounting Standards Board (FASB) in 1972, and in the UK with the ASB in 1990. In Australia a governmental standard-setting body (AARB) was merged with the professional equivalent in 1988, effectively leaving the profession in control because it appoints four of the nine members of the AARB and provides technical and administrative support.

A classification of accounting rule-making for nine countries could be presented as in Figure 2. In the UK the position until 1981 was as for New Zealand; that is, company law with few accounting rules except disclosure requirements, plus more detailed accounting standards. The 1981 and 1989 UK Companies Acts introduced a large number of accounting rules from Directives of the EC, created by an institution with philosophical roots on the right of Figure 2. Nevertheless, most of the detail in the UK can still be found in standards. Although these are now produced by the independent ASB, members of the profession are heavily represented on this body, and the profession is the main enforcement mechanism for standards. The introduction in the 1989 act of the possibility of civil action by the Review Panel against directors has as its nearest analogy the Enterprise Chamber in the Netherlands which creates precedents by hearing accounting cases.

Current standards and their status

The ASB has adopted the former ASC's standards (Statement of Standard Accounting Practice – SSAP) and has issued some of its own (Financial Reporting Standard – FRS). A list of these standards is shown in Appendix 3. SSAPs will be progressively withdrawn and replaced by FRSS. The status of these standards is that they would generally be considered by a court as necessary rules to be followed in company annual accounts in order for these to give a true and fair view. The latter requirement is the overriding legal instruction. The standards are also backed by the accountancy bodies, whose members are the auditors of companies. In general, auditors are required to mention non-compliance with standards in their audit reports if the directors do not make explanations. The auditors must state if the accounts do not, in their opinion, give a true and fair view.

Institutional arrangements

Financial Reporting Council (FRC) A trust with 30 members who are generally very senior representatives from the City, industry and the profession. The FRC meets a few times each year. It has an overseeing and fund-raising role.

Accounting Standards Board (ASB) The board issues standards on its own authority. It has two full-time members, including its chairman, eight

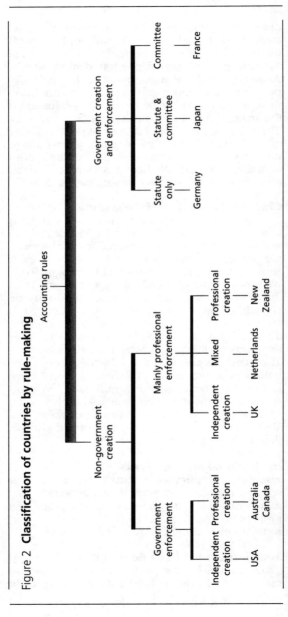

Figure 2 **Classification of countries by rule-making**

part-time members and two government observers.

Review Panel   There are 17 members chaired by a QC. The members are similar in seniority and mix to the FRC. The panel's task is to identify companies whose accounts do not comply with the Companies Act and to institute civil actions, possibly resulting in the directors having to revise accounts at their personal expense.

Urgent Issues Task Force (UITF)   A 15-member committee of the ASB whose task is to examine issues covered by law or standards but where there are unsatisfactory or conflicting interpretations. The purpose is to establish a consensus answer before bad accounting or non-standard accounting is established. Its published conclusions will not have the status of standards but, if broken, will require a qualified audit report.

Legal position

- Legal recognition for ASB (as issuer of standards), FRC (as overseer of issuing of standards), Review Panel (as investigator and applicant to court).
- Requirement for directors of public and large private companies to state whether accounts comply with standards and to give particulars of departures from standards.

A psychological change

These changes to the position of accounting standards marked a major shift from the 1980s to the 1990s: out went wheeler-dealing *laissez-faire*, in came conceptually based rules with some enforcement mechanism. This change was, of course, typical of many which hit the City in the post-Thatcher years.

In the 1980s it was commonly believed that company directors could (and should?) engage in clever accounting schemes to mislead the market. Auditors were seen to be in the pockets of directors and to have little desire and less power to oppose "commercially sensible" accounting practices rather than transparent ones. It was the era of Maxwell, of the Guinness affair and of off-balance sheet financing.

However, in the 1990s there have been examples of dramatic falls in share price after Review Panel investigations, and even of the removal of auditors for agreeing with the directors on an issue which later gave rise to investigation. This is in contrast to the 1980s when auditors were removed for disagreeing with the directors.

A further sign of a tougher regime is the ability of the ASB to stick to its guns over some difficult issues. For example, in September 1994 the ASB issued FRS 7, *Fair Values in Acquisition Accounting*. This makes demands on the subject of the calculation of goodwill (see next essay) which were highly unpopular with finance directors. In the old days of the ASC such an unpopular standard would almost certainly not have been issued.

One member of the ASB (a finance director) issued a dissenting opinion; and it is notable that the ASB's members were increased to ten after this by the addition of another finance director. Could this have been an attempt, by the mysterious powers who choose ASB members, to dilute the ASB's reforming zeal?

Incidentally, FRS 7 received a very good press, and the unpopularity was confined to the preparers of the accounts, not the users.

International pressures

International standard-setting arrangements were discussed at the beginning of this essay. By the late 1990s there was considerable pressure on the ASB to bring UK accounting into line with the rules of the International Accounting Standards Committee (see page 20). However, the UK is a member of the board of the IASC and the ASB's thinking has influenced the IASC.

ACCOUNTING FOR GOODWILL AND BRANDS

This issue has perhaps been the most controversial UK accounting problem over the last decade. Goodwill is the amount paid for an entity or a set of assets in excess of the value of the individual items bought. In the context of group accounting, goodwill on consolidation is the excess of the cost of buying the shares in a subsidiary over the fair value of its separable net assets. "Fair value" generally means the amount that would have to be paid for the assets if they were currently bought individually. "Separable net assets" means the identifiable tangible and intangible assets less the liabilities.

Some argument surrounds the calculation of fair values, and in particular whether anticipated expenses of reorganisation, redundancy, and so on should be taken into account. Companies are keen to do the latter because the expenses then avoid the profit and loss account in future years.

The latest document on this subject is FRS 7 of late 1994. This demands that the determination of fair value should not be done from an acquirer's perspective. That is, the fair valuation should not include the anticipated closing down of factories, provisions for the sacking of staff, or proposed changes of use of assets. Fair value should be that which a free market would arrive at. The result is that the total fair value of assets is generally higher than in the past, and goodwill is lower. This means that subsequent depreciation is higher and subsequent sales of assets seem to yield less profit. It also means, for example, that directors have to charge redundancy expenses next year rather than as part of the goodwill calculation. All in all, it is a rigorous requirement, even compared with that of the United States.

The major controversy concerns the treatment of goodwill once calculated. UK practice over the last decade (as approved by SSAP 22) was to write off goodwill immediately against reserves. This avoids having a nebulous asset in the balance sheet but, mainly, it avoids having to depreciate the asset against income over an arbitrary period. Of course this makes profits look larger. However, there are several disadvantages to this treatment.

1 Many acquisitions involve a large amount of goodwill. To write this off immediately appears to show that money has been thrown away. It also leads to a large hole in the balance sheet where the goodwill would have been. An illustration of this is shown in Table 1, where Marks & Spencer's group accounts show smaller net assets than the parent. Since the group includes the parent, this is counter-intuitive (in other words, daft). The explanation is largely seen in the "profit and loss account" reserve, which is smaller for the group because of goodwill write-offs. This problem did not occur in 1996 or 1997. Some companies have filled the hole by estimating a value for "brand names". Since there is no accounting standard on this topic, these intangible assets do not have to be depreciated.

2 By never showing an asset for goodwill and never showing an expense related to it, directors are not having to account for their spending. They also never have to show whether the goodwill has lost value. This seems like poor accountability.

3 This UK practice was out of line with many other countries (including the United States, France and Japan) and with the International Accounting Standards Committee.

An exposure draft (ED 47) of 1990 proposed to change UK practice but was met by a chorus of disapproval from finance directors. After that the Accounting Standards Board (ASB) kept quiet on the subject for several years. In December 1993 the ASB produced a discussion paper outlining six possible solutions.

In December 1997 FRS 10 was issued. This requires goodwill to be shown on balance sheets

Table 1 **Extract from the balance sheet of Marks & Spencer plc, March 31st 1995**

	The Group £m	The Company £m
Fixed assets		
Tangible assets:		
land and buildings	2,736	2,447
fixtures, fittings and equipment	522	395
assets in the course of construction	39	23
	3,297	2,865
Investments	43	775
	3,340	3,640
Current assets		
Stocks	377	255
Debtors: receivable within one year	578	1,194
receivable after more than one year	482	54
Investments	193	–
Cash at bank and in hand	736	57
	2,366	1,560
Current liabilities		
Creditors: amounts falling due within one year	1,364	982
Net current assets	1,002	578
Total assets less current liabilities	4,342	4,218
Creditors: amounts falling due		
after more than one year	568	250
Provisions for liabilities and charges	38	35
Net assets	3,736	3,933
Capital and reserves		
Called-up share capital	699	699
Share premium account	190	190
Revaluation reserve	455	464
Profit and loss account	2,371	2,580
Shareholders' funds (all equity)	3,715	3,933
Minority interests (all equity)	21	–
Total capital employed	3,736	3,933

like an asset. There is a "rebuttable presumption" that goodwill wears out (and should be amortised) over its useful life, which is up to 20 years. However, the presumption can be rebutted, even to the extent of claiming an infinite life. When a life exceeding 20 years is used there must be an annual test for impairment. Any impairment in value must be charged against income.

It remains to be seen whether most UK companies will take the "infinite life" route and avoid a goodwill expense, partly through the vagueness of the impairment test. However, balance sheet recognition of goodwill will reduce the international difference in practice. An important point is that UK companies are not required to go back and recover goodwill previously written off, so it will take years for the old difference to fade away.

FRS 10 applies the same rules to all other intangibles, so there now seems to be no advantage in relabelling goodwill as "brands".

INTERNATIONAL DIFFERENCES IN ACCOUNTING

International differences in financial reporting are as complex and profound as international differences in language or culture. For example, many readers will be aware that US and UK accounting rules and practices differ significantly. Nevertheless, in a world context US/UK accounting is similar, rather as the US/UK languages are. When dealing with France or Germany, the accounting is as different as the language. Going further from home, the complete incomprehensibility of the Japanese language to most of us is a useful clue to the difficulties of mastering Japanese accounting.

Some precise illustrations of international differences can be obtained from those companies which publish US GAAP figures as well as domestic figures. Here are some examples of earnings numbers, mostly for December 1996 year-ends.

	Domestic	US GAAP
Ericsson, Sweden (SKr m)	7,110	7,976
Glaxo-Wellcome, UK (£ m)	1,997	979
Alcatel Alsthom, France (Fr m)	2,725	(1,198)

Legal systems

There are several underlying causes of accounting differences. First, there are two main systems of law in the developed world. There is codified law, originally Roman law, which is a detailed scheme of laws and penalties, the basic stance being that there should be a law on any matter; and there is English (as opposed to British) law. The Plantagenet kings organised the English system of common law, equity, and case law. It rests on such concepts as "the reasonable man" and "the true and fair view".

Consequently, in much of continental Europe and Japan, it is clear that accounting is just another part of the law, requiring detailed rules from the state. However, to the British, accounting is not law but a mixture of art and science wherein highly trained professionals should be left to exercise their judgment (and charge their fees).

Different legal systems have different effects on accounting and until recently British, Irish, Australian and other law said virtually nothing about profits and values. This changed for the UK and Ireland in the 1980s as a result of the German-inspired EC Fourth Directive. In the United States there is no general legal framework for accounting.

Providers of finance

Second, the providers of finance and thus the users of accounting information differ markedly in different countries. In Germany bankers predominate. In France and Italy it is bankers, family businesses and the government. By contrast, private and institutional shareholders abound throughout the English-speaking world. The importance of loan finance in Germany may be demonstrated by average gearing ratios but there is an even simpler statistic in Table 2 (for exchanges with over 200 domestic listed companies and a market capitalisation over £150bn).

Before Spain entered the European Community, the UK had more listed companies than all the other countries of the EC added together. For more than a century, in the English-speaking world, outside shareholders have owned companies, thus requiring published information and auditors. On the other hand, continental bankers, families and governments get information by having representatives on boards of directors.

Influence of tax

Third, there is the importance of tax as a determinant of accounting rules. In the UK taxable profit is based on accounting profit with adjustments; accounting is not seriously interfered with by tax rules. In continental Europe, on the other hand, financial reporting was largely invented for the purposes of the tax collectors. Thus many rules of accounting have been determined by tax acts. In Germany, for example, depreciation is to be looked up in tax tables. In many continental

Table 2 **Major stock exchanges**

Exchange	Domestic companies	Market capitalisation as % of UK
Europe		
Paris	710	35
German Exchanges	437	41
Amsterdam	217	20
London	2,303	100
North America		
Toronto	1,196	26
NASDAQ	4,760	82
New York	2,428	410
Asia		
Hong Kong	518	22
Tokyo	1,714	252
Australasia		
Australian	1,129	18
Africa		
Johannesburg	614	20

Source: Based on *London Stock Exchange Fact Book*, 1996.

countries, where 100% depreciation allowances are given as investment incentives in some circumstances, these must be taken for accounting as well as tax purposes. This will result in new assets being valued at zero in balance sheets, which is not "true and fair" to a British person but is normal to a German.

Accountants
The last general difference is in the auditing profession. The professional bodies are affected by accounting differences but they also perpetuate them. For example, when Italy wished dramatically to change its accounting from 1975 onwards,

Table 3 **Some public accountancy bodies, age and size**

Country	Body	Founding date[a]	Approx. number 1997 ('000)
US	American Institute of Certified Public Accountants	1887	328
Canada	Canadian Institute of Chartered Accountants	1902 (1880)	60
UK	Institute of Chartered Accountants in England & Wales	1880 (1870)	112
	Institute of Chartered Accountants of Scotland	1951 (1854)	14
	Association of Chartered Certified Accountants	1939 (1891)	53
	Institute of Chartered Accountants in Ireland	1888	10
Australia	Australian Society of Certified Practising Accountants	1952 (1887)	83
	Institute of Chartered Accountants in Australia	1928 (1886)	29
New Zealand	New Zealand Society of Accountants	1909 (1894)	23
Netherlands	Nederlands Instituut van Registeraccountants	1895	10
France	Ordre des Experts Comptables et des Comptables Agréés	1942	15
Germany	Institut der Wirtschaftsprüfer	1932	8
Japan	Japanese Institute of Certified Public Accountants	1948	12

a Dates of earliest predecessor bodies in brackets.

it had to use Anglo-American accounting firms to do it. Table 3 shows the size and age of professional bodies whose members can be auditors. The small number of German auditors compared with those of the United States, for example, is partly explained by the existence of a recent second-tier body in Germany, and by some more complications of comparison. However, a large part of the difference is due to the comparative lack of importance of external audit in Germany.

Eight examples of difference

1 The degree to which accountants and auditors search for fairness as opposed to correctness or legality has differed substantially. A dominance of outside shareholders as financiers and a lack of interference by company or tax laws have been associated with the demand for fairness in the UK and the Netherlands. The gradual implementation of the EC's Fourth Directive has introduced the related *image fidèle* and so on into continental statutes. However, most of Europe is reacting to this by increasing disclosures rather than by changing the numbers given in financial statements.

2 In some countries the effects of taxation rules on detailed practices of depreciation, bad debt provisions and asset valuations are great. However, in the UK, the United States and the Netherlands, most accounting values and measurements are not seriously affected by taxation requirements.

3 The degree of conservatism is greater in Germany than in the UK. This may be because of the different mix of users of financial statements (for example banks are important in Germany) and the desire for objectivity in financial statements on which tax is exactly based. Conservatism expresses itself in the lack of capitalisation of development expenditure, the strictness of historical cost, the use of replacement cost when it is the lowest valuation of inventories, the establishment of statutory reserves and the maintenance of lavish provisions for contingencies.

4 The prevalence of provisions as distinct from reserves has been a feature of continental Europe. Provisions for contingencies are not only an example of conservatism, they also allow companies to smooth income, particularly when added to the practice of omitting depreciation charges in bad years. For countries where the main users are long-run financiers, smoothing may be a sensible practice, but it makes international profit comparisons dangerous.

5 The predominant valuation bases vary greatly internationally, as does the degree of experimentation with supplementary information. In Germany and Japan, it seems inevitable that the required method of valuation is a strict form of historical cost, so that tax values will be objective and auditable. At the other extreme is the Netherlands, the only European country where historical cost was under serious threat. In France, Spain and Italy, where there is much tax and other government influence, there has also been more inflation than in Germany and a greater drive towards the creation of large and efficient equity capital markets. Governments and stock exchange bodies in these countries have appreciated the effects of inflation on historical cost accounting and have required revaluations.

6 The prevalence of consolidation has varied dramatically. In the United States and the UK consolidation gradually became normal in the early decades of this century, because of the predominance of shareholders, the complex structures of businesses and the absence of inflexible laws. In Germany and France some consolidation has been practised since the 1960s, but full-blown rules were not put in place until the late 1980s. In some other European countries consolidation is still a rarity. The rules for equity accounting, for goodwill measurement and depreciation, and for merger accounting, also differ greatly.

7 The degree of uniformity varies internationally. In countries like Germany, with detailed rules for public companies that are obeyed, there is uniformity of presentation in the financial statements of different companies. In France the *plan comptable* imposes uniformity for internal accounting as well as for published financial statements. Belgium, Spain and Greece are following the idea of a plan at least for external reporting. There is now some uniformity imposed by the Fourth Directive in the UK and the Netherlands.

8 Lastly, it is possible to discern a difference in the extent of shareholder orientation in the presentation of financial statements. In the UK there is a predominant use of the vertical format that allows net working capital, net assets and shareholders' funds to be shown. Italy's two-sided double-entry format, however, does not allow this. Until 1993 year-ends, it also showed the current profit at the base of the liabilities side, current losses as an asset, and bad debt and depreciation provisions as liabilities. These are good pieces of double-entry logic, but they are not best designed to tell the readers about the company's financial position.

Dangerous comparisons
The differences discussed above are so large that it is clearly dangerous to compare sets of accounts from different countries without making significant adjustments. Harmonisation is proceeding, but slowly (see next essay). One of the problems is the deep-seated nature of the causes of the differences in accounting practices.

TOWARDS GREATER HARMONY

If the United States, the UK and Australia tried to reduce accounting differences they would be likely to set up a committee of accountants and to issue professionally set standards (it would be called the International Accounting Standards Committee; be founded in 1973 after a conference in Sydney; be based in London; use English as its only official language; and have had Canadian, Australian and British Secretaries General). By contrast, if the Commission of the European Union (EU) wished to reduce accounting differences, it would operate through legislation, and the main accounting Directive would be drafted in the late 1960s by a German auditor.

To harmonise or to standardise

"Harmonisation" is a process of increasing the compatibility of accounting practices by limiting their degree of variation. "Standardisation" appears to imply the imposition of a more rigid and narrow set of rules. However, within accounting these two words have almost become technical terms, and you cannot rely upon the normal difference in their meanings. Harmonisation is a word that tends to be associated with the transnational legislation being promulgated by the EU; standardisation is a word often associated with the International Accounting Standards Committee (IASC).

International professional standardisation is designed to help preparers and auditors of the financial statements of multinationals. By contrast, EU governmental harmonisation was intended for the protection of investors. To achieve this and to promote the movement of capital in the "common market", it is necessary to create a flow of reliable, homogeneous financial information from companies throughout the EU. Auditors and preparers of financial statements, and investors who rely on their statements, suffer from the existence of significant international accounting differences:

either ignorance of the differences leads to wrong decisions, or awareness of the differences leads to avoidance of foreign involvement or to expensive adjustment procedures.

Sovereign problems
The most fundamental obstacle to harmonisation is the size of the present differences between the accounting practices of different countries. Using the type of classification of accounting systems outlined in Table 4, there are several significant differences even within the Anglo-Saxon class, let alone between that class and the continental one. These latter differences go to the root of the reasons for the preparation of accounting information. The general dichotomy between shareholder/fair view presentation and creditor/tax/conservative presentation is an obstacle sufficiently difficult not to be overcome without major changes in attitudes and law. Indeed, it is not clear that it should be overcome. If the predominant purposes of financial reporting vary by country, it seems reasonable that the reporting should vary, at least for domestic purposes.

Another obstacle is the lack of strong professional accountancy bodies in some countries. This means that any organisation such as the IASC, which seeks to operate through national accountancy bodies, will not be effective in all countries. The alternative to this, a worldwide enforcement agency, is also lacking.

A further problem is nationalism. This may show itself in an unwillingness to accept compromises that involve changing accounting practices towards those of other countries. This unwillingness may exist on the part of accountants and companies or on the part of states that may not wish to lose their sovereignty. Another manifestation of nationalism may be the lack of knowledge or interest in accounting elsewhere. A rather more subtle and acceptable variety of this is the concern that it would be difficult to alter internationally set standards in response to a change of mind or a change of circumstances.

Table 4 **A two-group classification**

Anglo-Saxon	Continental
Background	
English law	Roman law
Large, old, strong profession	Small, young, weak profession
Large stock exchange	Small stock exchange
General accounting features	
Fair	Legal
Shareholder-orientation	Creditor-orientation
Disclosure	Secrecy
Tax rules separate	Tax-dominated
Substance over form	Form over substance
Professional standards	Government rules
Specific accounting features	
Percentage of completion method	Completed contract method
Depreciation over useful lives	Depreciation by tax rules
No legal reserves	Legal reserves
Finance leases capitalised	No lease capitalisation
Funds flow statements	No funds flow statements
Earnings per share disclosed	No earnings per share disclosures
No secret reserves	Secret reserves
No tax-induced provisions	Tax-induced provisions
Preliminary expenses written off	Preliminary expenses capitalisable
Taking gains on unsettled foreign currency monetary items	Deferring gains on unsettled foreign currency monetary items
Some examples of countries[a]	
UK	France
US	Germany
Canada	Austria
Australia	Sweden
New Zealand	Italy
Hong Kong	Portugal
Singapore	Japan
Denmark	Belgium
Netherlands	Greece

a Some countries on the right began to move left in the 1980s, particularly for the consolidated accounts of listed companies. France and Sweden are examples of this.

Overcoming the obstacles

The IASC works through the issue of non-binding professionally set standards, containing many options. Although the IASC is an Anglo-Saxon idea, all major developed countries now belong to it, as do many developing countries. In many of the countries in the left-hand column of Table 4 compliance with domestic rules will generally ensure compliance or, at least, not be incompatible with most IASC rules. In some developing countries IASC standards have been adopted or adapted. In some countries in the right-hand column, such as Italy, IASC standards are used for the group accounts of listed companies for matters where no government rules apply. However, in some of these countries elements of IASC standards are against national law or practice.

The European Commission achieves its harmonising objectives mainly through directives, which must be incorporated into the laws of member states. First, the commission, which is the EU's permanent civil service, decides on a project and asks an expert to prepare a report. The Council of Ministers, consisting of the relevant ministers from each EU country, decides (usually unanimously) if a directive is to be adopted. In the case of a directive, member states are required to introduce a national law within a specified period, although they often exceed it, as discussed below.

In order to achieve political consensus in difficult areas, the directives contain many options and many omissions. For example, goodwill can be either capitalised or immediately written off against reserves, and currency translation is not dealt with at all. There are dozens of provisions in the directives that begin with such expressions as "member states may require or permit companies to…". So the exact effects of any directive on a particular country will depend upon the laws passed by national legislatures.

The two main accounting directives are the fourth and the seventh which are now implemented in all EU countries. The fourth is based on the German public companies act (Aktiengesetz) of 1965. It introduces standardised formats for financial statements (with some options) and extends the scope of publication and audit to all but small private companies (generally those with fewer than 50 employees). There are also many disclosure requirements and, new for the law of Anglo-Saxon countries, accounting valuation and measurement rules. The directive has reduced the European differences in that, for example, the UK has gained standardised formats and legal valuation rules; France has gained extra disclosure requirements and the "true and fair view"; and Germany has increased its audit and publication requirements. However, despite the universal imposition of the "true and fair view" and many detailed valuation rules, the previous differences in national measurement practices (see Table 4) have largely survived.

The Seventh Directive has arguably been more successful. Many EU countries had no group accounting at all (for example Portugal) or had it only for public companies (for example Germany). The implementation of the directive makes group accounting obligatory for all public companies and for other groups with over 500 employees. This is a dramatic advance in the publication of group accounts. Furthermore, although there are some optional elements, the definition of subsidiaries and associates and the technical details of consolidation are largely standard.

Two noticeable areas of difference are permitted:

- the use of proportional consolidation for joint ventures, which is required in France, optional in most countries, but illegal in the UK, except for unincorporated joint ventures; and
- the treatment of goodwill, which must be amortised over five years in Spain, but can be amortised over longer periods or immediately written off against reserves in most countries.

One important effect of the Seventh Directive

in some countries is that an opportunity has been grasped to liberate the group accounts from some of the effects of tax-based valuation principles. For example, in France and Spain, several of the accounting features on the right of Table 4 still apply to the financial statements of individual companies but do not apply to the group accounts of listed companies: leases may be capitalised, gains taken on unsettled foreign currency items, and so on.

Spare the rod, rely on commercial sense

The directives have been criticised for being slow and for ossifying practices, since it is virtually impossible to amend a directive. Consequently, the European Commission announced in 1990 that there would be no more directives on accounting. Further progress may be left up to the IASC and to commercial pressures that cause large companies to adopt international accounting practices in order to seek finance on international markets.

By the late 1990s a number of large European companies had begun to prepare consolidated financial statements according to IASC rules. Also, the standard-setters in several countries (particularly in Africa and Asia) had decided to base their standards closely on those of the IASC.

In 1998 the IASC was finishing off a series of new and revised standards designed to satisfy IOSCO, the world's stockmarket regulators. If this works, IOSCO may agree to the use of the IASC's standards for foreign companies on all the world's stock exchanges.

Part 2
A–Z

AAA
See AMERICAN ACCOUNTING ASSOCIATION.

ABOVE THE LINE
An expression relating to the PROFIT AND LOSS ACCOUNT or INCOME STATEMENT. The line in question is the NET PROFIT, or the PROFIT on ordinary activities after taxation, of such statements. BELOW-THE-LINE amounts are appropriations such as DIVIDENDS. Thus above-the-line amounts is are EXPENSES or REVENUES of the business. EARNINGS PER SHARE figures are calculated excluding below-the-line amounts.

ABSORPTION COSTING
The allocation of all FIXED COSTS and VARIABLE COSTS in the calculation of the cost of goods or services produced.

ACCELERATED DEPRECIATION
DEPRECIATION at a faster rate than would be suggested by an even allocation of cost over an asset's expected life. This is most commonly found in the context of tax concessions designed to encourage investment. For the calculation of TAXABLE INCOME in such cases, businesses would be allowed to depreciate certain ASSETS (such as energy-saving devices or assets in depressed regions) more quickly than accountants otherwise would. This occurs in many countries; see CAPITAL ALLOWANCES for the UK system.

ACCOUNTABILITY
See STEWARDSHIP.

An accountant's is a sensible yet glamorous occupation.
John Braine, *Room at the Top*, 1957, ch. 2

ACCOUNTANCY
The terms accountancy and accounting are used interchangeably by many people. However, they might say "the ACCOUNTANCY PROFESSION" but "MANAGEMENT ACCOUNTING"; the former is often associ-

ated with the profession and the latter with the subject matter, particularly in the context of education or theory. Accounting includes mechanical aspects such as DOUBLE ENTRY book-keeping, which might be said to be part of FINANCIAL ACCOUNTING. The latter also involves the preparation, presentation and interpretation of financial statements. Management accounting is more concerned with the use of accounting data for decision-making and control by managers.

ACCOUNTANCY PROFESSION

Accountancy is an exceptionally old occupation. However, the oldest professional bodies of accountants were formed in the 1850s in Edinburgh and Glasgow. Shortly afterwards there was similar activity throughout the English-speaking world, and eventually elsewhere. (For more information on the UK bodies see CONSULTATIVE COMMITTEE OF ACCOUNTANCY BODIES.) The professional bodies set standards of entry for training; operate training and examination systems; and make ethical and technical rules. The profession is also organised at an international level (see FÉDÉRATION DES EXPERTS COMPTABLES EUROPÉENS and INTERNATIONAL FEDERATION OF ACCOUNTANTS).

> *We have no desire to say anything that might tend to encourage women to embark on accountancy, for although women might make excellent book-keepers, there is much in accountancy proper that is, we think, unsuitable for them.*
> Council of the Institute of Chartered Accountants in England and Wales, *The Accountant*, September 14th 1912, p. 341

ACCOUNTANTS INTERNATIONAL STUDY GROUP

Founded in 1966, the Accountants International Study Group (AISG) comprised members from professional ACCOUNTANCY bodies in the UK, the United States and Canada. It was set up to study and report on accounting practices in the three countries. Twenty studies were issued, mainly on financial reporting matters, such as INVENTORIES (1968), CONSOLIDATED FINANCIAL STATEMENTS (1972) and INTERIM REPORT (1975). The AISG was wound up in 1977 when the INTERNATIONAL FEDERATION OF ACCOUNTANTS was formed.

ACCOUNT DAY
The day on which dealers in STOCKS and SHARES have to settle their bills. The period varies from one STOCK EXCHANGE to another.

ACCOUNTING
See ACCOUNTANCY.

ACCOUNTING CONCEPT
An expression commonly used for the fundamental conceptual rules of accounting (see ACCOUNTING PRINCIPLES).

ACCOUNTING CONVENTION
Another expression commonly used for the fundamental conceptual rules of accounting (see ACCOUNTING PRINCIPLES).

ACCOUNTING EQUATION
An algebraic representation of a summary of what happens in the DOUBLE ENTRY system. The BALANCE SHEET might be expressed as $A_0 = L_0 + C_0$ (that is, total ASSETS at time zero equal total LIABILITIES and CAPITAL at time zero). The capital figure grows from time zero to time one by the earning of profit for the period; that is, $C_0 + P_1 = C_1$ (Equation 2). The profit (P_1) is made up of the total REVENUES less the total EXPENSES of the period: that is, $P_1 = R_1 - E_1$ (Equation 3). It is, of course, also the case that $A_1 = L_1 + C_1$ (Equation 4).

So inserting Equation 3 in Equation 2 gives:
$$C_1 = C_0 + R_1 - E_1$$
Inserting this in Equation 4 gives:
$$A_1 = L_1 + C_0 + R_1 - E_1$$
Rearranging this gives:
$$A_1 + E_1 = L_1 + C_0 + R_1$$
That is, the items on the left (assets and expenses) are all the debits, which are seen to equal the

items on the right (liabilities, capital and revenues) which are all the credits. This is a basic principle of double entry.

ACCOUNTING PERIOD
See FINANCIAL YEAR.

ACCOUNTING PLANS
These are detailed rules for the maintenance of BOOK-KEEPING records and the preparation of annual financial reports. The plans are issued by government-controlled committees. Several European countries, including France and Spain, use such plans.

ACCOUNTING POLICIES
The detailed methods of valuation, measurement and recognition which a particular COMPANY has chosen from those generally accepted by law, ACCOUNTING STANDARDS or commercial practice. These policies must be used consistently, and must be disclosed (this is required in the UK, for example, by the accounting standard SSAP 2 and by COMPANY LAW). A company's ANNUAL REPORT will include a "statement of accounting policies" that have been applied in the financial statements.

Examples of disclosure of policies would include whether a company was using STRAIGHT-LINE DEPRECIATION or REDUCING BALANCE DEPRECIATION; whether it was using FIRST IN, FIRST OUT (FIFO) or AVERAGE COST for the valuation of STOCKS (INVENTORIES); and how it was treating provisions for future pension payments.

ACCOUNTING PRINCIPLES
The word "principles" poses a slight problem in accounting. In the United States it usually means conventions of practice, whereas in the UK it means something more fundamental and theoretical. Thus the US GENERALLY ACCEPTED ACCOUNTING PRINCIPLES encompass a wide range of broad and detailed accounting rules of practice. In the UK the detailed rules are often called practices, policies or bases; and broader matters such as ACCRU-

ALS or PRUDENCE were traditionally referred to as concepts or conventions.

However, perhaps because lawyers (and those in Brussels at that) were involved in the drafting of the EC's Fourth DIRECTIVE which led to the 1981 Companies Act in the UK, British usage is now more confused. The 1981 act referred to five broad "principles" of accounting: GOING CONCERN, CONSISTENCY, PRUDENCE, accruals (MATCHING) and individual valuation. The first four were all to be found in the UK's SSAP 2, described as "concepts".

The problem with these broad principles in any country is the possibility of conflict. For example, in a going concern, the matching concept suggests that development costs ought to be carried forward and matched against the future REVENUES that they are designed to create (see RESEARCH AND DEVELOPMENT). However, prudence suggests that, because it is possible that no benefits will arise, all R&D costs should be immediately charged as EXPENSES. This would also lead to greater consistency. The same applies to advertising expenditure.

In the United States CONSERVATISM and consistency win in the shape of SFAS 2, which does not allow the CAPITALISATION of R&D costs. In the UK the initial exposure draft (ED 14) followed that precedent, but after complaints from heavy R&D spenders, ED 17 and the subsequent SSAP 13 allowed capitalisation of development expenditure under prudent conditions.

Under SSAP 2 prudence is required to override other conventions when there is conflict. Under UK COMPANY LAW no such provision exists. It is fortunate, then, that these mandatory principles are vague and may be broken in (disclosed) special circumstances or in order to allow a TRUE AND FAIR VIEW.

There are many other accounting conventions, such as MATERIALITY and MONEY MEASUREMENT.

ACCOUNTING PRINCIPLES BOARD

Set up in the United States in 1959 by the AMERICAN INSTITUTE OF CPAS (AICPA), the Accounting Principles

Board (APB) replaced the AICPA's Committee on Accounting Procedure, which between 1939 and 1959 had issued 51 ACCOUNTING RESEARCH BULLETINS. The APB was itself replaced in 1973 by the FINANCIAL ACCOUNTING STANDARDS BOARD (FASB).

The APB issued 31 "Opinions" and four "Statements". In many cases these have not been replaced by subsequent standards, and thus remain part of GENERALLY ACCEPTED ACCOUNTING PRINCIPLES.

The demise of the APB followed the setting up of two committees by the AICPA to investigate deficiencies in the rule-making procedures. One source of dissatisfaction was alleged dominance by large accountancy firms. A report by the Wheat Committee in 1972 led to the setting up of the FASB. Another problem was seen to be the lack of a CONCEPTUAL FRAMEWORK. The Trueblood Committee's report led to the FASB's major project designed to establish such a framework.

ACCOUNTING RATE OF RETURN
See RATE OF RETURN.

ACCOUNTING RECORDS
See BOOKS.

ACCOUNTING RESEARCH BULLETINS
Documents produced between 1939 and 1959 by the Committee on Accounting Procedure of the AMERICAN INSTITUTE OF CPAS. There were 51 such bulletins, some of which have not been superseded by the publications of the ACCOUNTING PRINCIPLES BOARD or the FINANCIAL ACCOUNTING STANDARDS BOARD.

ACCOUNTING STANDARDS
Technical accounting rules of valuation, measurement, recognition and disclosure. The exact title of accounting standards varies from country to country. The practical use of the term seems to have originated officially with the Accounting Standards Steering Committee (later the ACCOUNTING STANDARDS COMMITTEE) in the UK in 1970. Stand-

ards in the UK are called STATEMENTS OF STANDARD ACCOUNTING PRACTICE and (from 1990) FINANCIAL REPORTING STANDARDS. In the United States STATEMENTS OF FINANCIAL ACCOUNTING STANDARDS have been issued by the FINANCIAL ACCOUNTING STANDARDS BOARD (FASB) since its foundation in 1973.

In the UK the standards are backed by the professional bodies of accountants to which auditors of companies belong. The standards are designed to be used in the preparation of all financial statements intended to give a TRUE AND FAIR VIEW, and the latter is required by COMPANY LAW for all companies. The sanction for a COMPANY whose directors break standards is a qualification of the AUDIT REPORT. The standards would also be persuasive in a court of law that was determining whether a set of financial statements gave a true and fair view.

In the United States the standards of the FASB form part of GENERALLY ACCEPTED ACCOUNTING PRINCIPLES, which are insisted upon by the SECURITIES AND EXCHANGE COMMISSION (SEC). Thus they have greater force than UK standards, but only for the comparatively small proportion of companies registered with the SEC. In Canada the professionally set standards are given legal backing.

Standards are often criticised for being inconsistent with each other and for not being based on a CONCEPTUAL FRAMEWORK. They may be criticised by practical accountants for constraining the room to manoeuvre or to give a fair view; and by the financial press and users for still allowing too much room for arbitrary or misleading accounting practices.

ACCOUNTING STANDARDS BOARD

A UK body which has set ACCOUNTING STANDARDS since 1990. Like the FINANCIAL ACCOUNTING STANDARDS BOARD in the United States, the Accounting Standards Board (ASB) is independent from (though influenced by) the accountancy profession and the government.

ACCOUNTING STANDARDS COMMITTEE

A UK body that set ACCOUNTING STANDARDS until 1990. The Accounting Standards Committee (ASC) was set up in 1970 (and known until 1976 as the Accounting Standards Steering Committee) by the Institute of Chartered Accountants in England and Wales (ICAEW) and soon joined by the five other major UK and Irish accountancy bodies: the Institute of Chartered Accountants of Scotland, the Institute of Chartered Accountants in Ireland, the Association of Chartered Certified Accountants, the Chartered Institute of Management Accountants and the Chartered Institute of Public Finance and Accountancy.

The ASC was set up because of a gradual loss of confidence in the profession's technical rules, caused partly by several scandals and catastrophes. For example, in October 1967, during a contested takeover by GEC, Associated Electrical Industries Ltd (AEI) forecast a profit of £10m for 1967. In July 1968 a loss of £4.5m was reported instead. Accounting for the difference, the former joint auditors of AEI attributed "roughly £5m to adverse differences which are matters substantially of fact rather than judgment and the balance of some £9.5m to adjustments which remain substantially matters of judgment". Other disquieting events were the collapse of Rolls Razor and the bid by Leasco Data Processing Equipment Corporation for Pergamon Press Ltd.

At the end of 1969 the ICAEW published a "Statement of Intent on Accounting Standards in the 1970s", which led to the formation of what was to become the ASC. The ASC was replaced by the ACCOUNTING STANDARDS BOARD in 1990 after a review of its operations.

ACCOUNTS

Records of all the BOOK-KEEPING entries relating to a particular item. For example, the wages account would record all the payments of wages. An account in the DOUBLE ENTRY system has a DEBIT side (left) and a CREDIT side (right). Often accounts are referred to as T-accounts, because of the rulings on the page that divide the left from the right and underline the title. A business may have thousands of accounts, including one for each debtor and creditor.

In the early days of accounting there were only personal accounts (for people who owed and were owed money). Later there were "real" accounts for property of various sorts; and "nominal" accounts for impersonal, unreal items such as wages and electricity. Accounts may be collected together in groups in ledgers or BOOKS of account.

In the UK accounts may also mean financial statements, such as the BALANCE SHEET and PROFIT AND LOSS ACCOUNT.

A tradesman's books [of account] are his repeating clock, which upon all occasions are to tell him how he goes on, and how things stand with him in the world; there he will know when 'tis time to go on, or when 'tis time to give over... His books being so essential to his trade, he that comes out of his time without a perfect knowledge of the method of book-keeping, like a bride undrest, *is not ready to be married; he knows not what to do, or what step to take.*

Daniel Defoe (c.1660–1731), *The Complete English Tradesman*, 2nd ed., 1727, vol. I, letter XX

ACCOUNTS PAYABLE
A US expression for CREDITORS.

ACCOUNTS RECEIVABLE
A US expression for DEBTORS.

ACCRUALS CONCEPT
An expression used to describe the standard practice whereby EXPENSES or REVENUES are included in the ACCOUNTS of the period to which they relate rather than of the period in which cash is paid or received. It is also known as the MATCHING principle, particularly in North America.

ACCRUED EXPENSES

Those EXPENSES which relate to a year but will not be paid until the following year. They result from the need regularly to draw up financial statements at a fixed time (for example, at the end of a COMPANY's year). During a year electricity will be used or properties will be rented, yet at the year end the related bills may not have been paid. These accrued expenses are charged against INCOME by accountants even though cash has not been paid nor perhaps the bills received. The DOUBLE ENTRY for these is the creation of CURRENT LIABILITIES on the BALANCE SHEET, which are the CREDIT corresponding to the DEBIT accrued expenses. This practice may apply also to wages and salaries, taxes, and so on. An allocation of amounts to "this year" and "next year" may be necessary where a supplier's account straddles two accounting years. The practice is an example of the use of the MATCHING concept.

ACCUMULATED DEPRECIATION

The total amount by which the accounting value of FIXED ASSETS has so far been reduced to take account of the fact that they are wearing out or becoming obsolete (see DEPRECIATION).

ACID TEST

See QUICK RATIO.

ACQUISITION

The normal method of BUSINESS COMBINATION (see CONSOLIDATED FINANCIAL STATEMENTS). In the United States this is called a purchase.

ACT

See ADVANCE CORPORATION TAX.

ADVANCE CORPORATION TAX

Part of the UK and Irish CORPORATION TAX system. As its name suggests, it is an advance payment of part of the corporation tax liability of a COMPANY. Advance corporation tax (ACT) is triggered by the payment of DIVIDENDS, and its size is proportionate to the size of the dividend. In 1997 plans to abolish ACT were announced.

AG
See *AKTIENGESELLSCHAFT*.

---

*Now it was a little astounding, and one could not
help wondering, whether those who managed big
companies did not forget sometimes that the body
of directors of the company were the agents of the
shareholders, that they owed them full
information subject to proper commercial and
reasonable necessities, and it was the
shareholders' interest they had to study. They
were not to regard shareholders as sheep who
might look up if they were not fed.*

Mr Justice Wright, *The Accountant*, August 8th 1931, p. 237

AGENCY THEORY
An application in accounting research of theories from economics and the behavioural sciences. It is suggested that directors and other managers (the agents), particularly those of a large COMPANY, have many other aims than that of maximising the long-run wealth of the owners of the company, the shareholders (the principals). Thus the behaviour of managers with respect, for example, to dividend policy or the choice of accounting policies will only be predictable by assuming self-interest and studying what that would lead to.

When it comes to choosing accounting policies or to lobbying for or against particular changes in ACCOUNTING STANDARDS, managers may consider the effects of the change on declared PROFIT figures. This may involve them in considerations of the effects on their compensation schemes or their reputations as managers if profits seem too large. The problem of the inefficiencies that may result from the separation of management from ownership is also important in more general considerations of the theory of the behaviour of companies.

AGM

See ANNUAL GENERAL MEETING.

AICPA

See AMERICAN INSTITUTE OF CPAS.

AISG

See ACCOUNTANTS INTERNATIONAL STUDY GROUP.

AKTIENGESELLSCHAFT

A German or Swiss PUBLIC COMPANY. *Aktiengesellschaft* (AG) literally means a SHARES company. There are about 2,000 such companies in Germany, which is very few compared with the number of UK public companies.

ALLOWANCES

A US expression for PROVISIONS, that is the amounts charged against PROFIT in anticipation of reductions in value (for an example see BAD DEBTS).

AMERICAN ACCOUNTING ASSOCIATION

A body whose primary membership is accounting academics in the United States. It organises large conferences each summer in a North American city, at which research is discussed and university recruitment carried out. It also publishes the prestigious academic journals, *The Accounting Review* and *Accounting Horizons*.

AMERICAN INSTITUTE OF CPAS

The American Institute of Certified Public Accountants (AICPA) was founded in 1887. It has approximately 330,000 members. It is responsible for ethical guidance for the profession; for setting AUDITING standards that lead to GENERALLY ACCEPTED AUDITING STANDARDS; and for an examination system. Until 1973 it was also responsible for ACCOUNTING STANDARDS, but that role has now been taken over by the FINANCIAL ACCOUNTING STANDARDS BOARD. However, the AICPA still provides comment on the agenda and exposure drafts of the standard-setters.

Just as companies in the United States must be

registered by state rather than federally, so CPAs must belong to a state body of CPAs. The total number of such CPAs somewhat exceeds those who have joined the AICPA. The rules for entry to the state CPA societies varies from state to state.

He was a CPA [certified public accountant] and looked it every inch. He even had ink on his fingers and there were four pencils in the pocket of his open vest.
Raymond Chandler (1888–1959), *The Lady in the Lake*, 1943

AMORTISATION
A word used, particularly in North America, to refer to certain types of DEPRECIATION, mainly that owing to the passing of time.

ANALYTICAL REVIEW
One method of audit testing, used as a complement to computations, verbal enquiries, inspection of records, and so on. It involves the review of financial statements, accounting records and other documents for unusual items or for the reasonableness of totals. The auditor should ensure that the financial statements show a picture consistent with his or her knowledge of the underlying circumstances of the business.

ANGLO-SAXON ACCOUNTING
Although financial reporting practices in the English-speaking world vary from country to country, just as the use of the language does, they all have a common origin and a common philosophy. As with the predominant language, the financial reporting practices of the United States, Canada, Australia, New Zealand and Ireland are British in origin. In the case of the US, the practices of London, Manchester, Glasgow and Edinburgh were exported in the late 19th and early 20th centuries in the most obvious of ways: the emigration of British accountants. For example, Arthur Young and James Marwick (names incorporated in BIG FIVE firms) moved from Glasgow to the US.

Perhaps the most obvious common characteristic is the emphasis on FAIR PRESENTATION. In the United States and Canada this is expressed as a requirement for financial statements to be fairly presented. In the other countries listed above, the requirement is to show a TRUE AND FAIR VIEW. This includes the use of several of the ACCOUNTING PRINCIPLES mentioned under that heading, and also substantial use of the concept of MATERIALITY, whereby unimportant amounts are not shown or not necessarily treated exactly correctly. Another relevant expression here is SUBSTANCE OVER FORM, whereby figures are shown in accordance with economic reality rather than legal form.

The Netherlands also has accounting of a similar type, as of course do many members of the British Commonwealth. The obvious contrast is the legal/tax basis of accounting in Germany.

The differences between these two main types of accounting probably arise from the English common law system (as opposed to codified continental law), the importance of private shareholders as providers of finance (as opposed to bankers and governments), and the lack of importance of tax rules for financial reporting in the Anglo-Saxon world.

ANNUAL GENERAL MEETING

A meeting of the shareholders of a COMPANY held once a year. To be more exact, under UK law, there must be a gap of no more than 18 months between annual general meetings (AGMs). At the meeting shareholders may:

- question directors on the contents of the ANNUAL REPORT and financial statements;
- vote on the directors' recommendation for a DIVIDEND;
- vote on replacements for retiring members of the board;
- conduct other business within the rules laid down by their company's MEMORANDUM OF ASSOCIATION and ARTICLES OF ASSOCIATION.

Under certain conditions, usually some sort of crisis, an EXTRAORDINARY GENERAL MEETING may be held at the request of the directors or shareholders.

The equivalent American expression is "annual meeting of stockholders".

ANNUAL REPORT

A document sent to shareholders after a COMPANY's year end. It must contain a report by the directors, the financial statements and notes, and the report of the auditors. Most large companies also include a less formal report in the form of a chairman's statement.

APB

See ACCOUNTING PRINCIPLES BOARD.

APPRECIATION

An increase in value (usually NET REALISABLE VALUE) of an asset. Under a strict HISTORICAL COST ACCOUNTING system, such appreciation is not recognised in the accounting records of the business until the asset is sold and the gain is realised. This is the case in the United States, Japan and Germany, and the practice is followed partly because of CONSERVATISM and partly because of the need for OBJECTIVITY; before the asset is sold it is impossible to be sure exactly what its market value is. Also, in a GOING CONCERN, the market value of FIXED ASSETS is not necessarily of interest to the users of financial statements. However, most systems of INFLATION ACCOUNTING make adjustments to asset values to record appreciation.

In the UK and several other countries the rules about recognising appreciation are more permissive (see REVALUATION).

APPROPRIATION ACCOUNT

An expression sometimes used to describe that part of the PROFIT AND LOSS ACCOUNT where the NET PROFIT for the year is appropriated to the owners or ploughed back into the business. Appropriations are, then, ways of using up PROFIT once it has been calculated. DIVIDENDS are appropriations, as are transfers to various RESERVES. Thus these amounts are not EXPENSES of the running of the business. It is not clear whether to regard taxation as an expense or as an appropriation, but it is generally treated as an expense.

In the published financial statements of a UK COMPANY, appropriations are made as a continuation of the profit and loss account. In the financial statements of a PARTNERSHIP the appropriation account will normally be a more obviously separate account, including of course the splitting up of the profit among the various partners.

In the United States the expression "statement of retained earnings" is more usual.

ARTICLES OF ASSOCIATION

A document drawn up at the foundation of a COMPANY, setting out the rights and duties of the shareholders and directors, and the relationship between one class of shareholder and another. (See also MEMORANDUM OF ASSOCIATION.) In the United States similar rules will be found in the BYLAWS.

ASB

See ACCOUNTING STANDARDS BOARD.

ASC

See ACCOUNTING STANDARDS COMMITTEE.

ASSETS

Generally things owned or controlled that have future economic benefits. However, it is in fact exceptionally difficult to define exactly what an accountant means by an asset. Various attempts have been made, principally in the United States. A definition is contained in part of the CONCEPTUAL FRAMEWORK project in the US (in Statement of Financial Accounting Concepts 3). According to that document the existence of an asset relies upon "probable future economic benefits obtained or controlled by a particular entity as a result of past transactions or events".

When all the assets in the BALANCE SHEET are added together, the result will be the total assets.

When the amounts due to outsiders (the LIABIL-ITIES) are deducted, what remains is the NET ASSETS or net worth of the business. Of course, because of the unrecorded assets and the sometimes curious valuation conventions of accountants, the "net worth" is probably much less than the business is worth (see below and ASSET VALUATION).

There are several problems with the definition of assets. For example, is a machine which is on a long LEASE to be considered as an asset of the lessee? Legally it still belongs to the lessor, but in many cases the economic substance of the initial leasing transaction is similar to a purchase plus a loan. In recent years the practice in the United States and the UK has moved towards treating many leased assets as belonging to the lessee.

A second example is a new road. It may be of great benefit to a COMPANY, and some of the company's taxes may have helped to pay for it. Also the company has rights to its use. However, the road does not belong to the company and is fairly clearly not the company's asset. Equally straightforwardly, a company may spend a lot of money drilling for oil, only to discover that it is a "dry hole". Since it will bring no future benefits, it is not counted as an asset.

In the case of some companies, such as Marks & Spencer or McDonald's, the most important assets do not appear on the balance sheet at all. The value of such companies rests on their future earning power which rests upon customer loyalty, brand names, trained staff, skilled management, and so on. These items are generally not treated as assets by accountants because their valuation would not be objective. It is not at all clear exactly what they are worth or exactly what has been spent to create them. Yet they are owned, they will bring future benefit, and amounts are constantly expended to create or preserve them. However, when a business is sold, an amount in excess of the accounting value of the assets may be paid. In the financial statements of the purchaser, this excess may be recorded as an asset called GOODWILL.

Thus the accounting definition of an asset is heavily hemmed in by a number of conventions, all of which have good reasons behind them. However, the net result is not necessarily easily comprehensible or satisfactory.

ASSET-STRIPPING
Asset-stripping or financial surgery was popular in the late 1960s and early 1970s. It is normally associated with the purchase of a business by financial entrepreneurs who have calculated that the asking price for the business as a GOING CONCERN is lower than the total amount that could be raised by selling the ASSETS separately.

ASSET VALUATION
The traditional method of valuation in accounting is HISTORICAL COST ACCOUNTING, whereby ASSETS are valued at purchase price or production cost, less DEPRECIATION (that is, at NET HISTORICAL COST). There are good reasons for this, such as CONSERVATISM and a desire for OBJECTIVITY. However, particularly when prices have risen, the historical cost of an asset may be misleading, given that many non-accountants assume that assets are recorded at a market price. In some countries, including the UK but not the United States, land and buildings are sometimes revalued to reflect the increase in what they could be sold for. The problem is that there are few rules: some companies revalue annually, some every five years, some never.

FIXED ASSETS other than land and buildings tend to be more uniformly shown at net historical cost, but it should be remembered that depreciation is not an exact measurement.

CURRENT ASSETS are valued at the lower of cost and NET REALISABLE VALUE, although in North America replacement cost is used where it is even lower. DEBTORS are valued at what the lender prudently expects to receive, and cash is valued at its face value.

ASSOCIATED COMPANY
A UK term for a COMPANY over which another has

significant influence. The equity method, which is described below, is used to account for such companies in their CONSOLIDATED FINANCIAL STATEMENTS. An enterprise will be presumed to be an associate if it is owned to the extent of 20–50%. Above 50% ownership it becomes a SUBSIDIARY; under 20% ownership it normally becomes a trade investment. A company held as a JOINT VENTURE with other owners will be treated as an associated company in the UK or the United States.

The equity method, as used in consolidated financial statements, involves recording the associate in the BALANCE SHEET as a single line called "investment in associated undertakings". This is valued at the cost of the investment in the associate at the time of purchase plus the appropriate proportion of the undistributed PROFIT made by the associate since that date (in the UK the cost will be split into the appropriate proportion of the FAIR VALUE of the assets and the implied GOODWILL).

DIVIDENDS passing from the associated company to its owner group cause cash to increase and investment in associated undertakings to decrease by the same amount. Profits earned by the associate cause the owner's consolidated profits to be increased by the appropriate share, and investment in associated undertakings to rise by the same amount.

AUDIT COMMITTEE

A committee to which a COMPANY's external auditors report. The committee's members are generally non-executive directors of the company.

An auditor is not bound to be a detective... He is a watch-dog, but not a bloodhound.
Lord Justice Lopes (1828–99), In re *Kingston Cotton Mill Co.* (no. 2), 1896

AUDITING

The basic aim of a modern audit in the UK or the United States is to give an opinion on whether the financial statements drawn up by the directors of a COMPANY give a FAIR PRESENTATION (in the US) or a TRUE AND FAIR VIEW (in the UK). In order to do this the auditors need to check the physical existence and valuation of important ASSETS and to examine the systems of INTERNAL CONTROL to ensure that transactions are likely to have been recorded correctly. If internal control is poor they will ask for it to be improved and increase the amount of checking done on sample transactions. If the control systems look good, small samples of various types of transactions may be checked.

The auditors would generally be expected to circularise a sample of some of the DEBTORS to confirm that they exist. They would normally attend the annual stock take (the count of the inventory in the US). They would try to spot and to question unusual items in the BOOKS of account or financial statements. The rules for auditing vary from firm to firm, but are to some extent found in AUDITING STANDARDS.

The directors and auditors will be hoping that the AUDIT REPORT can be "unqualified" as a result of the relevant laws and standards being followed, and the overall impression of a fair view being given. In order to achieve this the auditors will try to persuade the directors to make any necessary changes to the published ACCOUNTS.

Auditing is an ancient activity. It means "hearing" (audit is derived from the Latin for "he hears"). Auditing was thus originally the process whereby the owner heard the account given by his steward of the use of the owner's resources for a period (see STEWARDSHIP). By the 19th century the many owners of a large company would appoint one of their number to be a specific auditor of the financial statements prepared by the directors whom they had appointed to manage the company. This was partly because the process of auditing had become more complicated as business itself became more complicated.

In the UK audit became compulsory for limited liability banks as a result of the 1879 Companies

Act which followed the spectacular failure of the City of Glasgow Bank in 1878. The 1900 Companies Act made audit compulsory for all companies. In the United States audit is compulsory for those companies registered with the SECURITIES AND EXCHANGE COMMISSION.

The qualifications that auditors must have are also set down: membership of a CPA body in the US, or in the UK membership of one of four bodies of the CONSULTATIVE COMMITTEE OF THE ACCOUNTANCY BODIES (or some other individuals recognised by the relevant government department). This provides a large amount of government-required work for accountants of recognised institutes. It is the single most important type of work for the members of these bodies, although many members do work in other fields. Auditing has become so complex that high standards of training are necessary. Both entry standards and examinations are now of high quality.

In Anglo-Saxon countries auditing is carried out by individuals or by firms which vary greatly in size. Some firms have hundreds of partners and thousands of staff. However, the audit is always the ultimate responsibility of a member of one of the appropriate professional bodies. (See also INTERNAL AUDIT.)

> *All in all, he looked the typical youngish chartered accountant of ability whose intelligence was so absorbed by his work that there was none left over for anything else.*
> Bruce Marshall, *The Bank Audit*, 1958, ch. 1

AUDITING PRACTICES BOARD
The committee of the CONSULTATIVE COMMITTEE OF THE ACCOUNTANCY BODIES that is responsible for preparing AUDITING STANDARDS and guidelines in the UK.

AUDITING STANDARDS
Rules for the practice of auditors which detail the

work to be covered by an audit and the standard practice for the AUDIT REPORT. The UK rules are drawn up by the AUDITING PRACTICES BOARD.

AUDIT REPORT

The report of independent auditors that is required on all annual financial statements of companies in the UK, and all those registered with the SECURITIES AND EXCHANGE COMMISSION in the United States.

In the United States reference is made in audit reports to FAIR PRESENTATION, GENERALLY ACCEPTED ACCOUNTING PRINCIPLES, consistency of application and GENERALLY ACCEPTED AUDITING STANDARDS. In the UK reference is made to COMPANY LAW and to a TRUE AND FAIR VIEW; compliance with ACCOUNTING STANDARDS is implied unless there is a statement to the contrary.

AUTHORISED SHARE CAPITAL

The maximum amount of a particular type of share in a particular COMPANY that may be issued. The amount is laid down in the company's MEMORANDUM OF ASSOCIATION.

AVCO

See AVERAGE COST.

AVERAGE COST

In the context of valuation of STOCKS (INVENTORIES), average cost (AVCO) is a method of determining the historical COST of a particular type of stock. As its name suggests, the cost of any unit of stock or material used is deemed to be the average of the unit costs at which the stock was bought. The average can be worked out at set intervals or each time there is a further purchase. Average cost is a minority practice in the UK and the United States.

BACKLOG DEPRECIATION

If a COMPANY bases DEPRECIATION on current values, backlog depreciation is the amount of extra depreciation that would be necessary in a particular year to make up for the fact that previous years' depreciation provisions had been based on values that are now out-of-date.

BAD DEBTS

Amounts of DEBTORS (ACCOUNTS RECEIVABLE) that have become or are expected to become uncollectable. There are various levels of bad debt. Normally, a person or COMPANY would hope and expect that a great majority of debts would eventually be paid. However, CONSERVATISM requires that all reasonably likely losses be anticipated. Thus:

- debts which are almost certainly uncollectable are deducted from the total;
- debts which are reasonably likely to be uncollectable have a specific provision (in the UK) or allowance (in the United States) made against them; and
- a general provision or allowance is made against the remaining debts based on previous experience with unexpected bad debts.

In each of the three cases there will be an expense charged against INCOME, and a reduction in the figure for debtors or accounts receivable shown on the BALANCE SHEET.

BALANCE SHEET

A snapshot of the accounting records of ASSETS, LIABILITIES and CAPITAL of a business at a particular moment, most obviously the accounting year end. The balance sheet is the longest-established of the main financial statements produced by a business. As its name suggests, it is a sheet of the balances from the DOUBLE ENTRY system at a particular time. It is important to note that it is probably not an indication of what the business is worth. This is because not all the business's items of value are recognised by accountants as assets, and because the ASSET VALUATION methods used are normally based on past costs rather than on present market values.

Initially, the balance sheet was not designed as a statement of worth at all; it was merely a mechanical by-product of the periodical closing of books in the double-entry system. (In one sense the balance sheet is the graveyard of the double-entry system; it balances because the double-entry system creates equal totals of debits and credits.) The worth of a business was more sensibly calculated by taking a quite separate inventory of all the assets and liabilities at a particular date.

Annual balance sheets are compulsory requirements of COMPANY LAW (in the UK) and the SECURITIES AND EXCHANGE COMMISSION (in the US).

Before the 1981 Companies Act in the UK (and still in some other English-speaking countries) formats and terminology varied substantially. In the United States many balance sheets use an "account format" with assets on the left and capital and liabilities on the right. The CURRENT ASSETS are shown above the FIXED ASSETS (see Table 5). Even the title of the balance sheet may be expressed differently; for example, "statement of financial position".

In the UK, account form balance sheets were the norm until the second half of the 20th century and are still used by partnerships and sole traders. Unlike US and continental European balance sheets, the assets were on the right and the capital and liabilities on the left.

However, long before the 1981 Companies Act, large companies in the UK had taken to using a statement (or vertical) format. This allows the presentation of NET CURRENT ASSETS (or working capital), and avoids the confusion that undistributed PROFIT might appear to be a liability. UK COMPANY LAW (now the 1985 Companies Act) sets out two balance sheet formats and allows companies to choose, although they must be consistent, between them. One format is shown in Table 6.

Table 5 **A US account form balance sheet**

JCN Inc
Balance Sheet, 31st December 199X ($'000)

Current assets		**Current liabilities**	
Cash	300	Loans payable	800
Accounts receivable	1,850	Accounts payable	1,200
Inventories	1,500	Accrued expenses	400
Total	3,650	Dividends	600
		Total	3,000
Investments	800	Deferred taxes	500
Properties		Long-term debt	3,000
Land	2,000	**Shareholders' equity**	
Buildings	2,000	Common stock	1,500
Machinery	3,000	Paid-in capital	500
		Retained earnings	2,950
Total	7,000	Total	4,950
Total assets	**11,450**	Total liabilities and equity	**11,450**

The other format has similar headings but is in account form, with the assets on the left, starting with fixed assets. The headings (as in Table 6) must be shown in the order laid down. There is a further level of subheadings which must be shown either on the balance sheet or, where clearer, in the notes to the balance sheet. The notes will also include other compulsory disclosures connected with balance sheet items, like cumulative amounts of DEPRECIATION. (See also CAPITAL COMMITMENTS and CONTINGENT LIABILITIES.)

> *It sounds extraordinary but it's a fact that balance sheets can make fascinating reading.*
> Mary Archer, "Quote Unquote", *Independent*, January 7th 1989

BANKRUPTCY

Individuals are insolvent if they are unable to pay their debts as they fall due. CREDITORS may sue for bankruptcy so that a court may declare the person

Table 6 **A UK statement form balance sheet**

D & D Pirana plc
Balance Sheet, 31st December 199X (£'000)

Fixed assets

Tangible assets:			
Land and buildings			4,000
Plant and machinery			2,000
Fixtures and fittings			<u>1,000</u>
			7,000
Investments			<u>800</u>
Total			7,800

Current assets

Stocks	1,500		
Debtors	1,850		
Cash at bank and in hand	<u>300</u>		
		3,650	

Creditors falling due within one year

Bank loans and overdrafts	800		
Trade creditors	1,200		
Corporation tax	800		
Proposed dividends	600		
Accruals	<u>100</u>		
		<u>3,500</u>	
Net current assets			<u>150</u>
Total assets less current liabilities			<u>7,950</u>

Creditors falling due after one year

Debenture loans			3,000

Capital and reserves

Called-up share capital	1,500		
Share premium	500		
Profit and loss account	<u>2,950</u>		
Shareholders' interest			<u>4,950</u>
Long-term liabilities and capital			<u>7,950</u>

legally bankrupt which will affect his or her ability to undertake commercial transactions. (See also INSOLVENCY.)

> *The whole affairs in bankruptcy have been handed over to an ignorant set of men called accountants, which is one of the greatest abuses ever introduced into law.*
> Mr Justice Quain in A.H. Woolf, *A Short History of Accountants and Accountancy*, 1912, p. 177

BEAR
An investor on a STOCK EXCHANGE who anticipates a fall in prices. A bear market is a pessimistic state of affairs at a stock exchange. The opposite is a BULL, who charges ahead, anticipating price rises (see also STAG). Successful bears are those who agree to "sell" shares that they do not yet own, in order to cover the sale by buying later when the price has fallen.

BELOW THE LINE
The line in question is that showing the NET PROFIT after tax in a PROFIT AND LOSS ACCOUNT (in the UK) or the NET INCOME in an INCOME STATEMENT (in the United States). (See ABOVE THE LINE.)

BETA
The beta coefficient of a share is an indication of one aspect of the risk attached to it. The beta shows the sensitivity of the price of a share to changes in the price of SHARES generally. (See CAPITAL ASSET PRICING MODEL.)

BIG FIVE
An expression used to describe the world's largest accounting firms, which have offices virtually throughout the world. In alphabetical order they are:

- Arthur Andersen
- Deloitte Touche Tohmatsu
- Ernst & Young

- Klynveld Peat Marwick Goerdeler (KPMG)
- PricewaterhouseCoopers

The order in which the firms ought to be listed depends on whether you count the number of offices, number of partners, number of staff, total fee INCOME, and so on. It also depends on which year, what the exchange rates are, whether it is for the world, the UK, the United States or some other context.

These firms are very well established throughout the Anglo-Saxon world, and increasingly in Europe. In some countries there is resistance to their success, and they have to operate under local names or have local partners, or they have to work through similar, legally separate, national firms.

Most of the firms started out in the UK and in the United States and later merged. The exception is Arthur Andersen, which has spread from the US. In many cases the founders of the US parts of these multinational firms were British expatriates. The role of such firms outside the UK and the US was originally to audit subsidiaries of UK or US multinationals. However, in many countries their work has now expanded to include much domestic AUDITING and consultancy.

The Big Five used to be the Big Six but Coopers & Lybrand merged with Price Waterhouse in July 1998 to form PricewaterhouseCoopers. The announcement of that decision to merge prompted Ernst & Young and KPMG to enter into merger talks but these came to nothing.

Chartered accountants in Edinburgh... must be like pretty prostitutes in Paris: a good one waiting under every other lamp-post.
Bruce Marshall, *The Bank Audit*, 1958, ch. 1

BILL OF EXCHANGE

An acknowledgement of debt, for example as a result of a non-cash trading transaction. A COMPANY may of course have "bills payable" or "bills receivable". Bills can be passed from one person to another; in other words they are negotiable. Banks may be willing to discount a bill, that is to give cash in exchange for the bill at a discount on its face value. The US expression is notes.

BONDS

A word used to cover many sorts of (usually) long-term loans to a COMPANY or other body (see DEBENTURES). The expressions "loan stock" or, in the United States, "obligations" or "debt" are also used. Bonds usually have a fixed life, a fixed INTEREST return and a fixed redemption value.

BONUS SHARES

SHARES issued to existing shareholders of a COMPANY in proportion to their shareholdings. Such shares are free, as their name suggests; no cash changes hands. The purpose is usually to lower the share price, perhaps for the psychological reason that it seems high in relation to other shares or has gone into two digits (that is, above £10 or $10). If a one-for-one issue is made the result would be a doubling of shares. Since nothing else about the company has changed, the share price ought to halve; but sometimes it falls less, perhaps because favourable attention is drawn to the company.

Accounting for the issue is straightforward; RESERVES of various kinds can be relabelled "share capital" to the total value of the PAR VALUE of the shares. Bonus issues are sometimes called scrip issues or CAPITALISATION issues (because reserves are being capitalised).

Next to being prepar'd for death, with respect to Heaven and his soul, a Tradesman should be always in state of preparation for Death, with respect to his books.
Daniel Defoe (c.1660–1731), *The Complete English Tradesman*, 2nd ed., 1727, vol. I, letter XX

BOOK-KEEPING

The day-to-day recording of transactions of a business or other body (see DOUBLE ENTRY for a detailed description). Book-keeping describes the more mechanical everyday aspects of accounting.

BOOKS

The detailed records of all the transactions of a business, kept on a daily basis. They include the ACCOUNTS. Some types of transactions are so numerous that the DOUBLE ENTRY system would be swamped if they were recorded individually; for example, CREDIT sales, credit purchases and cash transactions. For these, special subsidiary books (DAY BOOKS) are used to record all the details and then to pass summary totals through to the main system. Thus there may be a SALES day book, a purchases day book and a cash book.

The accounting records are sometimes divided up into ledgers of similar types. For example, there may be a sales ledger and a purchases ledger in which totals from the day book are "posted". Traditionally there would have been personal ledgers (for amounts owed to or by persons), real ledgers (for land, buildings, and so on) and nominal ledgers (for those things that were neither personal nor physical, such as INTEREST charges, DEPRECIATION, and so on). However, some people use the expression NOMINAL LEDGER to describe all the main accounts. Nowadays accounting records in many businesses are kept on computer files, so that physical books and ledgers are beginning to go the way of quill pens.

BOOK VALUE

The value of the ASSETS and LIABILITIES of a business, as held in its ACCOUNTS (see NET BOOK VALUE).

BUDGET

A financial plan, usually expressed in money terms and divided into periods. For example, a business may have a cash budget for the coming year, detailing the planned inflows and outflows of cash on a monthly basis. This will involve the calculation of the planned surplus cash at the end of each month. There will also be SALES, production, purchases, EXPENSES and other budgets. The purpose of a budgeting system is to help to plan, monitor and control the business throughout the year.

BULL

An investor on a STOCK EXCHANGE who anticipates a rise in prices. A bull market is an optimistic state of affairs at a stock exchange. Successful bulls are those who buy shares with the intention of selling them soon afterwards when prices have risen. The buying and selling may not be settled on the same day. Thus buying can be achieved without the apparently necessary resources. The opposite of a bull is a BEAR (see also STAG).

BUSINESS COMBINATION

An American expression for an ACQUISITION or merger involving two or more companies. The accounting treatments can be varied and complex (see CONSOLIDATED FINANCIAL STATEMENTS).

BUY-OUT

The purchase of a COMPANY by a group of people containing some of its former managers (see MANAGEMENT BUY-OUT).

BYLAWS

In the United States, the rules relating to the operation of an organisation. For UK companies these are called the ARTICLES OF ASSOCIATION.

CADBURY COMMITTEE

A UK committee which produced proposals for good corporate governance in 1993.

CALLED-UP SHARE CAPITAL

Newly issued SHARES are sometimes paid for in several instalments or calls. The called-up capital is the total amount of instalments so far due from all shareholders.

Capital is dead labour that, vampire-like, lives only by sucking living labour, and lives the more, the more labour it sucks.

Karl Marx (1818–83), *Das Kapital*, 1867, I

CAPITAL

A word used somewhat loosely in the business world in general, and even by accountants. It may mean the total of a COMPANY's finance, including all share capital, past profits, long-term loans and CURRENT LIABILITIES. Such an aggregation might be called total capital. It would, of course, equal total ASSETS.

However, capital might also be used to mean the long-term finance; that is, the above total less current liabilities. Yet another meaning might be all the elements of capital belonging to shareholders (shareholders' EQUITY); or even just the amount of money contributed in the past by the shareholders. Unfortunately, the reader will have to determine the exact meaning by the context. At least you have been warned.

The expression "capital employed" is also seen on balance sheets and in PROFITABILITY ratios. It usually means the total long-term capital, although such an aggregate might be called "net capital employed" because it does not include current liabilities.

CAPITAL ALLOWANCES

A system of DEPRECIATION used in the determination of TAXABLE INCOME that is unique to the UK and Ireland. The rates are specified in annual Finance Acts; they are often more generous than the depreciation that accountants would charge for financial accounting purposes. There are two main reasons for the existence of capital allowances. First, the subjective nature of depreciation is thereby removed from the tax system. Accountants can charge the most appropriate depreciation in their ACCOUNTS without being worried that it will affect taxation. In a sense, the reverse problem occurs in most continental countries, in that tax-based depreciation rates determine accounting depreciation. Second, generous capital allowances can be used as an investment incentive. This ACCELERATED DEPRECIATION for tax purposes lowers the tax bill quickly and thus is a cash incentive.

From 1986 in the UK there have been 25% annual WRITING DOWN ALLOWANCES for plant, cars, patents and know-how. The allowances work on a reducing balance basis. For industrial buildings there is a 4% allowance on a straight-line basis. However, there are no allowances for commercial buildings, such as shops and offices; or for land, which generally does not wear out.

When assets are sold, capital allowances are, in effect, reclaimed by the Inland Revenue to the extent that the sale price exceeds the tax written-down value, which will usually be zero for plant and machinery.

Capitalism without bankruptcy is like Christianity without hell.
Frank Borman, "Sayings of the Week", *Observer*, March 9th 1986

CAPITAL ASSET PRICING MODEL
A theory, which may be expressed by equations, about the determination of the price of marketable securities, such as SHARES in a LISTED COMPANY. The model is built up on a number of assumptions, some of which are not very realistic. It is designed to show, for a particular security, the relationship between its expected return and its risk. The total risk attached to a security can be broken down into systematic risk (related to the rest of the securities market) and unsystematic risk

(related only to the particular security). Systematic risk cannot be avoided by diversification, but unsystematic risk can be. The following equation describes the capital asset pricing model in algebraic terms:

$$E(R_j) = R_f + B_j (ER_M - R_f)$$

where $E(R_j)$ is the expected return on security j; R_f is the risk-free rate of return; B_j represents systematic risk (the BETA coefficient); and ER_M is the expected return on the market portfolio.

CAPITAL COMMITMENTS

Future commitments that will entail CAPITAL expenditure. For example, a COMPANY may have contracted to purchase, at a future date, a new office building. At the BALANCE SHEET date, it may have no asset and no liability or cash expended as a result of the commitment. However, the commitment may be of interest to users of financial statements, particularly those concerned with the LIQUIDITY of the company. Thus capital commitments are recorded in the notes to the balance sheet.

CAPITAL EMPLOYED

The aggregate finance used by a business. Sometimes the expression is used to refer to the total of all LIABILITIES and CAPITAL; sometimes it excludes CURRENT LIABILITIES (see CAPITAL).

CAPITAL GAINS TAX

A tax on the increase in value of certain ASSETS when realised. In the UK such a tax has operated on most assets since 1965, and has been indexed for inflation since 1982. For companies, capital gains are subject to CORPORATION TAX.

CAPITALISATION

There are three definitions:

1 The aggregate market price on a STOCK EXCHANGE of all the listed SHARES of a COMPANY, or perhaps all its ORDINARY SHARES. It is, in a sense, what the company is worth, which may considerably exceed the balance sheet NET ASSETS. This is because the BALANCE SHEET does not include all valuable ASSETS (for example, customer loyalty or trained staff), and because accounting ASSET VALUATION is often not based on market prices.

2 Recording COSTS as assets rather than as EXPENSES. For example, a company might capitalise RESEARCH AND DEVELOPMENT costs.

3 Using amounts of RETAINED PROFITS for the purpose of issuing more shares to existing share-holders.

CAPITALISATION ISSUE
See BONUS SHARES.

CAPITAL LEASE
US term for FINANCE LEASE.

CAPITAL MAINTENANCE
A concept used to determine the definition of PROFIT. It is variation in this that underlies the dif-ferences in systems of INFLATION ACCOUNTING.

Under HISTORICAL COST ACCOUNTING, the profit of a period is recognised as any excess of the money CAPITAL at the end of the period over the money cap-ital at the beginning of the period (after correcting for additions or reductions of capital, such as share issues or DIVIDENDS). However, it might well be argued that there is no real profit unless the share-holders' capital is maintained in real terms, that is after adjustment to take into account the fall in the value of money caused by inflation. An accounting system based on this concept of capital mainte-nance would be called current purchasing power (CPP) in the UK, or constant dollar accounting or general price level adjusted (GPLA) in the United States. Such systems use retail price indices to adjust accounting figures from historical cost. This is a fairly simple set of adjustments, which does take inflation into account. It was the method favoured by the professional accountancy bodies in the

English-speaking world in the late 1960s and early 1970s. In several highly inflationary economies, such as some in South America, CPP systems have been adopted.

An alternative view of the maintenance of capital is to concentrate neither on the shareholders' money capital (historical cost) nor on the shareholders' real capital (CPP), but on the physical capital of the business. This would be an ENTITY VIEW rather than a PROPRIETARY VIEW. This point of view is taken on the grounds that the business is a GOING CONCERN and does not intend to return capital to the shareholders. Thus for the decisions of managers and investors, the present worth, past progress and future prospects of a business can best be indicated by measuring current values and then calculating the resultant profit implications. A version of such a system called CURRENT COST ACCOUNTING was introduced as a requirement for supplementary financial statements of large and listed companies in the UK in 1980 (until 1985), although its exact capital maintenance concept is not crystal clear. Other English-speaking countries have adopted similar requirements. In the United States the SECURITIES AND EXCHANGE COMMISSION required disclosure of some replacement cost information. In the Netherlands some companies have been publishing replacement cost-based financial statements for decades.

Thus how exactly profit is measured depends upon which concept of capital is adopted.

CAPITAL REDEMPTION RESERVE
An amount of PROFIT set aside as undistributable when SHARES are bought back by a COMPANY.

CAPITAL RESERVES
Those ACCOUNTS representing amounts which are not legally distributable or are not intended to be distributed by a COMPANY. Examples of such RESERVES are:

- the SHARE PREMIUM account, which represents amounts paid in when shareholders bought

their shares from the company;
- the CAPITAL REDEMPTION RESERVE, which represents amounts that have been substituted for share CAPITAL when shares were redeemed from their owners by the company;
- the LEGAL RESERVE as required in many countries other than the UK or the US;
- the REVALUATION reserve, which represents increases in the value of ASSETS that have been recorded in the accounts but have not yet been realised by the sale of the assets.

These reserves, like all others in accounting, are not of course amounts of cash. The latter is an asset; the reserves are on the other side of a BALANCE SHEET showing, in a sense, to whom the assets belong. The reserves are part of shareholders' EQUITY. The equivalent US expression is RESTRICTED SURPLUS.

CARRYING VALUE
The amount at which an item is shown in a BALANCE SHEET. Depending on the country and the COMPANY, this might be a written-down value of depreciated historical cost or a more recent REVALUATION.

Pan Am takes good care of you. Marks & Spencer loves you. Securicor cares... At Amstrad: "We want your money".
Alan Sugar, "Sayings of the Week", *Observer*, May 3rd 1987

CASH FLOW
Sometimes used to refer loosely to the amount of cash coming into or going out of a business in a particular period. However, it can be used as a more precise accounting term, particularly in North America, to refer to NET PROFIT with DEPRECIATION charges added back. The latter will have been deducted in the calculation of the former, but is not of course a cash payment of the period in question.

CASH FLOW STATEMENT

One of the main annual financial statements in many countries, including the UK and the United States. This statement uses a cash basis rather than an accruals basis. It concentrates on the cash flows relating to operations, financing, investment, and so on.

CASH GENERATING UNIT

The smallest set of ASSETS for which it is possible to measure cash inflows and outflows separately. In a manufacturing industry, this might be a whole factory rather than an individual machine. An IMPAIRMENT is measured on the basis of cash generating units.

CCA

See CURRENT COST ACCOUNTING.

CCAB

See CONSULTATIVE COMMITTEE OF ACCOUNTANCY BODIES.

CHAIRMAN'S REPORT

A statement in the ANNUAL REPORT of most large UK companies in which the chairman of the board of directors reviews the progress of the past year and the prospects for the future. It will often contain acknowledgement of support from staff, suppliers, customers or shareholders; it may make some political points about taxation, investment or inflation. The report is not a mandatory requirement, thus it neither obeys particular rules nor follows a standard format.

CHART OF ACCOUNTS

A German invention that provides a detailed, standardised arrangement of account codes for ASSETS, LIABILITIES, CAPITAL, REVENUES and EXPENSES. The system may be decimalised, and varies industry by industry. Its original purpose was to allow companies to record and prepare accounting information in a uniform, and thus comparable, way. This would enable inter-firm comparisons to be made, and would enhance the efficiency of industry.

Charts were imposed as a uniform system in France during the second world war, and proved sufficiently successful to be adopted permanently as part of the PLAN COMPTABLE GÉNÉRAL (general accounting plan). Thus, throughout France, an auditor, a tax inspector or an industrialist can easily feel at home in a COMPANY's accounting system because uniform coding and definitions are in use.

In Germany there is a voluntary chart of accounts, which is still useful for its original purpose of inter-firm comparison.

CLOSE COMPANY

A COMPANY which is controlled by its directors or by five or fewer participators or their associates (that is, five or fewer shareholders or their families or partners). Such a company is likely, of course, to be small. It may be similar to a PARTNERSHIP in its management but is incorporated for legal and tax purposes. A LISTED COMPANY is required to note whether or not it is a close company in its ANNUAL REPORT. The term close company is defined in tax legislation and, under certain circumstances, involves a higher level of taxation.

CLOSING RATE METHOD

A UK term for the normal method of FOREIGN CURRENCY TRANSLATION, whereby the financial statements of foreign subsidiaries are translated into the parent's currency at current exchange rates.

COB

See COMMISSION DES OPÉRATIONS DE BOURSE.

CoCoA

See CONTINUOUSLY CONTEMPORARY ACCOUNTING.

COMMERCIAL CODE

Part of the legal system in most of continental Europe and in countries influenced by codified law, such as Japan. Commercial codes usually contain detailed accounting rules applying to enterprises. They are amended by companies acts or their equivalent.

COMMISSION DES OPÉRATIONS DE BOURSE

The approximate French equivalent of the SECURITIES AND EXCHANGE COMMISSION in the United States. The Commission des Opérations de Bourse (COB) was founded in 1968 by the French government and charged with supervising and improving the financial capital market. As with all continental European bourses, comparatively few shares are listed on the Paris Bourse. The government and banks are important providers of finance in France.

Perhaps the most obvious impact that the COB had on the financial reporting of French listed companies resulted from its campaign in favour of CONSOLIDATED FINANCIAL STATEMENTS. Consolidation was virtually unknown in France in 1968, but a majority of French listed companies prepared consolidated statements by the time it became compulsory for them in 1986.

COMMISSIONE NAZIONALE PER LE SOCIETÀ E LA BORSA

The approximate Italian equivalent of the SECURITIES AND EXCHANGE COMMISSION in the United States. The Commissione Nazionale per le Società e la Borsa (CONSOB) was founded in 1974, and has pushed accounting for listed companies towards ANGLO-SAXON ACCOUNTING.

COMMON STOCK

A US term for the ORDINARY SHARES in a corporation. Normally a majority of the ownership CAPITAL will comprise issues of common STOCK, although PREFERENCE SHARES are also issued. Stock usually has a PAR VALUE, which is little more than a label for the type of stock. The amount that would have to be paid for one share will be determined, in the case of a listed share, by the daily price on the STOCK EXCHANGE. The total of common stock is part of the SHAREHOLDERS' FUNDS of a COMPANY. The return to common stock is a dividend. In the long run the size of DIVIDENDS depends on the PROFIT-ABILITY of the company.

COMPANIES ACTS
See COMPANY LAW.

COMPANY
A business that is a legal entity separate from its owners, the shareholders. Thus companies can own ASSETS, they can sue and be sued at law, they can have "perpetual succession" (that is, there need be no limit to their lives, irrespective of the lives of, or changes to, the owners). Most companies have limited liability, which means that the owners of the company have limited liability for its debts. In effect the owners' liability is usually limited to their shareholdings. Because owners may be granted limited liability (in the case of the UK from the 1855 Companies Act onwards), many investors are prepared to risk their money and become co-owners. This enables very large amounts of CAPITAL to be raised, and therefore makes very large companies possible. If there were no limited liability (as with a PARTNERSHIP) it would be much more difficult to persuade investors to become co-owners, without their insisting on becoming co-managers so that they could safeguard their own investments and potential LIABILITIES. Most investors have no desire to become co-managers of businesses, and most businesses have no desire for vast numbers of co-managers. Thus limited liability is essential for large businesses.

Table 7 **Abbreviated company names**

	Private	*Public*
France	Sarl	SA
Germany	GmbH	AG
Italy	Srl	SpA
Japan	YK	KK
Netherlands	BV	NV
UK	Ltd	plc

Before the 1844 Companies Act in the UK it had been necessary to have an Act of Parliament or a Royal Charter in order to set up a company. Now companies are commonplace in the UK and throughout the world. They are set up with a series of legal transactions and registration with government (or state government) offices. In the UK the MEMORANDUM OF ASSOCIATION and ARTICLES OF ASSOCIATION outline the rules of the company; in the United States the analogous documents are the CERTIFICATE OF INCORPORATION and the BYLAWS.

Throughout much of the Western world (though not in the United States) the law distinguishes between a PRIVATE COMPANY and a PUBLIC COMPANY. Table 7 gives abbreviated designations in certain countries which are used as part of the names of companies.

It is necessary for a company to be public in order for there to be a market in its securities (SHARES or loans). The extreme example of a public market is a STOCK EXCHANGE listing. Thus public companies are generally larger than private companies. The law imposes greater restrictions on public companies. In the UK, for example, public companies must have a minimum issued capital of £50,000. The definition of DISTRIBUTABLE PROFIT is stricter for them. They are not allowed the exemptions from publication granted to certain private companies.

There are around 12,000 public companies in the UK, about half of them listed, and about 950,000 private companies. In some countries, such as Germany and the Netherlands, public companies are required to have two-tier boards, comprising a supervisory board (with some employee representation) and a management board. Proposals like this are contained in the draft Fifth DIRECTIVE of the EU.

In the United States there is no such legal distinction between public and private. However, the analogous companies to public ones are those that are registered with the SECURITIES AND EXCHANGE COMMISSION (SEC). Companies must register with the SEC in order for there to be a market in their securities. The SEC lays down audit and disclosure requirements. It also provides the backing for ACCOUNTING STANDARDS. Thus the rules for registered companies are much more extensive than those for unregistered companies. (See also CLOSE COMPANY and CORPORATION TAX.)

COMPANY LAW

In some countries, such as Germany, company law has been the main source of general and detailed requirements in accounting. In other countries, such as the United States, there is virtually nothing on accounting in state or federal law; instead accounting rules are set by the SECURITIES AND EXCHANGE COMMISSION, by an independent committee, by the profession, or by some combination of these. In the UK, before the EC's Fourth DIRECTIVE led to the provisions of the 1981 Companies Act, there were only general requirements in the law concerning accounting. For example, proper BOOKS of account had to be kept; annual financial statements had to be audited, to be published and to give a TRUE AND FAIR VIEW; and a number of detailed disclosures had to be made.

UK company law really began with the 1844 act which enabled companies to be easily formed, and the 1855 act which allowed limited liability. Compulsory independent audit for banks followed in 1879; and for all limited companies in 1900. Not until the 1929 act did profit and loss accounts become compulsory. Group accounts were required by the 1947 act (consolidated into the 1948 act).

Company law was consolidated again in the 1985 Companies Act. Before that the principal act of 1948 had been supplemented by acts in 1967, 1976, 1980 and 1981. The 1981 act added requirements for the formats of the BALANCE SHEET and the PROFIT AND LOSS ACCOUNT; extended disclosure requirements; provided certain exemptions from publication for smaller private companies; and introduced detailed compulsory ACCOUNTING PRINCIPLES. Many of these provisions came, via the

Fourth Directive, from German law (particularly the Public Companies Law of 1965). The 1989 Companies Act amended the 1985 act by implementing into UK law the requirements of the Seventh and Eighth Directives (on group accounting and on auditors).

On several matters other than accounting UK law has traditionally been fairly detailed. For example, there are many provisions on audit, directors' duties, rights of shareholders and CREDITORS, conduct of the ANNUAL GENERAL MEETING, and so on. The law also contains many provisions on business names and INSIDER DEALING.

COMPREHENSIVE INCOME

The INCOME of an entity for a period including all recognised gains and losses, not just those included in a conventional INCOME STATEMENT. In the United States, companies are required to disclose comprehensive income. In the UK, it can be seen in the STATEMENT OF TOTAL RECOGNISED GAINS AND LOSSES.

CONCEPTUAL FRAMEWORK

A theoretical structure to underlie the technical rules in accounting. One way to explain the idea of a conceptual framework is to refer to the efforts of the FINANCIAL ACCOUNTING STANDARDS BOARD in the United States, which began a conceptual framework project after the Trueblood Committee Report of 1973 criticised the ad hoc nature of accounting standards. The project has led to several STATEMENTS OF FINANCIAL ACCOUNTING CONCEPTS. The first concerned the objectives of financial statements. It was concluded that the most important aim was to provide shareholders with useful information for making financial decisions. Then the elements of financial statements were identified and defined. For example, ASSETS, LIABILITIES and INCOME were discussed. These are, of course, difficult to define with precision.

The third statement concerned the qualitative characteristics of accounting information. In order to achieve the desired objectives, it was concluded that relevance and reliability were the two most important features. Relevance would be determined with respect to the decisions to be made by users; reliability would increase with OBJECTIVITY.

The INTERNATIONAL ACCOUNTING STANDARDS COMMITTEE published a framework in 1989. The UK has published drafts of a statement of principles.

CONSERVATISM
See PRUDENCE.

CONSISTENCY
The concept that a COMPANY should use the same rules of measurement, valuation and recognition from year to year in its financial statements. This is now well established in most developed countries. A company may be allowed to make changes in special circumstances, such as an alteration in ACCOUNTING STANDARDS, but the change should always be disclosed in the ANNUAL REPORT. The purpose of consistency is to enable a better comparison of a year's profits and values with those of previous years. The concept that different companies should use the same rules to assist inter-company comparisons might be called UNIFORMITY. Consistency is required in the UK by accounting standards (SSAP 2) and by COMPANY LAW.

CONSOB
See COMMISSIONE NATIONALE PER LE SOCIETÀ E LA BORSA.

CONSOLIDATED FINANCIAL STATEMENTS
A means of presenting the financial position and results of a parent and its SUBSIDIARY companies as if they were a single entity. Consolidation ignores the separation of parents and subsidiaries because of legal and geographical factors and accounts for the group of companies as a single entity. The financial statements of all the companies in the group are added together, with adjustments to extract intra-group trading and indebtedness, to achieve FOREIGN CURRENCY TRANSLATION, and to ensure uniform ACCOUNTING POLICIES throughout.

CONSULTATIVE COMMITTEE OF ACCOUNTANCY BODIES

The Consultative Committee of Accountancy Bodies (CCAB) is a co-ordinating body set up by the six professional accountancy bodies in the UK and Ireland after proposals for their merger failed in 1970. These bodies, in order of size, are as follows.

Institution	Designatory letters
The Institute of Chartered Accountants in England and Wales (ICAEW)	ACA, FCA
The Association of Chartered Certified Accountants (ACCA)	ACCA, FCCA
The Chartered Institute of Management Accountants (CIMA)	ACMA, FCMA
The Institute of Chartered Accountants of Scotland (ICAS)	CA
The Chartered Institute of Public Finance and Accountancy (CIPFA)	IPFA
The Institute of Chartered Accountants in Ireland (ICAI)	ACA, FCA

A committee is a cul de sac down which ideas are lured and then quietly strangled.
Sir Barnett Cocks, *New Scientist*, November 8th 1973

CONTINGENCIES

These result from conditions that exist at a BALANCE SHEET date but where the outcome depends on uncertain future events. As part of CONSERVATISM, accountants recognise all reasonably probable losses relating to contingencies in advance. However, some losses are merely possible and are contingent upon some event, such as the loss of a law case or a debtor defaulting on a BILL OF EXCHANGE which the COMPANY has guaranteed. These contingencies are accounted for when a loss is probable. Otherwise, they are not accounted for, in the sense of adjusting the financial statements, but notes to the balance sheet will explain the cause of the contingency and the amount (or an estimate) of exposure.

CONTINUOUSLY CONTEMPORARY ACCOUNTING
Usually known by its acronym CoCoA, this is a
system of price-change adjusted accounting developed by Professor Ray Chambers of the University
of Sydney. Valuations under this system are based
on the selling price of ASSETS (their NET REALISABLE
VALUE).

CONVERTIBLE LOAN STOCK
Long-term debts, DEBENTURES or BONDS that are
convertible, at some future date at the option of
the lender, into equity, that is ORDINARY SHARES of
the borrowing COMPANY. This means that investors
can have the safety of debt finance (in that there
is fixed annual INTEREST, and preferential repayment of CAPITAL if a company is wound up), with
the PROFIT-sharing aspects of equity if the company does well. For the company the advantages
are that it will be easier to attract finance at a reasonable annual cost, and that the returns to the
providers of finance will initially be in the form of
interest, which is tax-deductible.

CORPORATION TAX
In the UK, corporation tax was introduced in 1965
as a separate tax on companies. Before that companies paid INCOME TAX on their business profits
(as sole traders and partnerships still do) plus a
special profits tax. In the United States companies
still pay income tax.

COSA
See COST OF SALES ADJUSTMENT.

COST
Valuation practices in many countries are based
on historical cost, that is the purchase price or
production cost of ASSETS. STOCKS (INVENTORIES) are
valued at the LOWER OF COST OR MARKET. Oil and gas
accounting is often based on a full cost method.
Cost can also be used to mean CURRENT REPLACE-
MENT COST.

The PROFIT of a business is calculated by setting the costs (or EXPENSES) of the period against its REVENUES. There are also many ways of analysing costs for COST ACCOUNTING or MANAGEMENT ACCOUNTING purposes.

> *Keeping accounts, Sir, is of no use when a man is spending his own money, and has nobody to whom he is to account. You won't eat less beef to-day, because you have written down what it cost yesterday.*
>
> Samuel Johnson (1709–84), Boswell's *Life of Johnson*, March 30th 1783

COST ACCOUNTING

The breaking down of various costs and REVENUES by product, location or manager. The purpose is to assist managers in working out which is the most profitable product, or which is the cheapest location, or how much should be charged for particular products.

COST OF SALES

The costs associated with making the products that have been sold in a period. This includes the appropriate proportions of production OVERHEADS, but not administration EXPENSES. It excludes the costs of unsold production. The cost of SALES is deducted from the sales revenue of the period in order to calculate gross PROFIT from trading.

The cost of sales is not the same as the purchases of materials for the period for two reasons: first, STOCKS (INVENTORIES) may have been built up or reduced during the period; second, work will probably have been carried out on the stocks during the period. Thus the cost of sales includes the factory wages and overheads. In order to adjust for stock changes, the calculation of the cost of sales is: opening stock plus purchases of materials and work done on the stock less closing stock.

COST OF SALES ADJUSTMENT

An amount used, in various systems of INFLATION

ACCOUNTING, to adjust the COST OF SALES for the extent to which its components have been affected by price changes. The calculation of the cost of sales includes figures for opening and closing STOCKS. The former will have been determined using stock prices current before the beginning of the year, and the latter using prices current before the end of the year. However, the purchases figure will normally be composed of various prices that amount to an average for the year. Thus several different price levels are involved in the cost of sales. The result is that the calculation does not give a good picture of the current cost of sales.

The cost of sales adjustment (COSA) is designed to correct for this. It is calculated by adjusting opening and closing stocks (and purchases, if necessary) to average-for-the-year prices. When prices are rising, the current cost of sales will be larger than the unadjusted cost of sales, so the difference (the COSA) will be an extra charge (a DEBIT) against PROFIT. Thus profit, adjusted for the COSA, will be smaller when prices are rising.

For which of you, intending to build a tower, sitteth not down first, and counteth the cost, whether he have sufficient to finish it?
Bible, Authorised Version, Luke 14:28

CPP
See CURRENT PURCHASING POWER ACCOUNTING.

CRC
See CURRENT REPLACEMENT COST.

CREATIVE ACCOUNTING
There is a well-known story about a large COMPANY that was interviewing several applicants for a senior accounting job. The applicants were given masses of accounting data and asked to calculate the PROFIT. The applicant who got the job was the one who asked: "What profit had you in mind?". There are so many subjective elements in the

measurement of value, or profit, that a wide range of answers is often legal and in conformity with GENERALLY ACCEPTED ACCOUNTING PRINCIPLES. Thus there is the opportunity to be creative. A rather more old-fashioned but similar expression is WINDOW DRESSING. Concern about these practices was one of the factors that led to the establishment of the bodies that set ACCOUNTING STANDARDS.

> *With "creative accountancy", who needs cheating?*
> Katharine Whitehorn, *Observer*, January 25th 1987

CREDIT

This word has two general meanings, although they both come from the same root. The origin is the Latin for "he believes" or "he trusts". When the only accounting records of a business were those of people who owed the business money, or were owed money by it, the simple entries would have been DEBIT for "he owes" and credit for "he trusts" or is owed. Thus a creditor is someone who is owed money.

As record-keeping developed into DOUBLE ENTRY, a debit and a credit were invented for all transactions. Thus, for example, a purchase of raw materials from a supplier who is not yet to be paid is recorded as: debit purchases, credit the supplier (the creditor). Similarly, a sale to a customer who is not yet to pay cash is recorded as: debit the customer (the debtor), credit SALES. In the full system, any increase in REVENUES, LIABILITIES or CAPITAL is a credit entry, as is any decrease in ASSETS or EXPENSES. If the system is working properly, the total of all the debits will equal the total of all the credits. The credit side of an account is conventionally the right-hand side.

The other meaning of credit is closely connected. To extend credit or to make sales on credit is to trust another person. The lender becomes the creditor, that is the one who trusts.

CREDITORS

As explained under CREDIT, a creditor is a "truster", someone to whom a business owes money. The US expression is accounts payable. Creditors are created by purchases "on credit" or by loans of various sorts. Short-term creditors are included under CURRENT LIABILITIES on a BALANCE SHEET; they are expected to be paid within the year. If credit purchases are the cause, the title used might be TRADE CREDITORS.

Long-term creditors are those who are not expected to be paid within the year. These might be trade creditors but are more likely to be holders of BONDS or DEBENTURES. The latter would normally be entitled to receive INTEREST, whereas trade creditors are not. However, trade creditors often offer discounts for prompt payment, which is an implied way of charging interest.

A tradesman's credit, and a maid's virtue, ought to be equally sacred from the tongues of men; and 'tis a very unhappy truth, that as times now go, they are neither of them regarded among us as they ought to be.
Daniel Defoe (c.1660–1731), *The Complete English Tradesman*, 2nd ed., 1727, vol. I, letter XV

CUM DIVIDEND

A share is bought cum dividend (or cum div) if the purchaser would receive the next payment of dividend. This is normal. The opposite is EX DIVIDEND, which may apply for a short period around the dividend date. In this case the seller keeps the next dividend, presumably to be received soon.

CUMULATIVE PREFERENCE SHARES

The normal types of PREFERENCE SHARES, on which any arrears of DIVIDENDS have to be settled before the ordinary shareholders can be paid a dividend.

CURRENCY TRANSLATION

See FOREIGN CURRENCY TRANSLATION.

CURRENT ASSETS

ASSETS which are intended for continuing use in the business. Such assets include STOCKS, DEBTORS and cash. A BALANCE SHEET may include current asset investments; that is, those designed to be held for a short period. Just as investments can be fixed or current, so automobiles can be fixed (if part of a fleet of COMPANY cars) or current (if part of the trading stock of a car dealer).

CURRENT COST ACCOUNTING

One of many possible systems designed to adjust accounting for changing prices. It is often included under the generic heading INFLATION ACCOUNTING, although it does not involve adjustments for inflation, but for specific price changes relating to the business's ASSETS. In the UK a standard (SSAP 16) was operational in the first half of the 1980s requiring supplementary current cost accounting (CCA) information from large companies.

Balance sheets under CCA contain assets which are normally valued at net CURRENT REPLACEMENT COST. This is what it would cost to buy an identical replacement (or, if necessary, a similar replacement after adjustment for the differences). The replacement cost is reduced to the extent that the asset has been depreciated, hence "net" current replacement cost. In practice, index numbers might be used as estimates for actual replacement costs.

A CCA PROFIT AND LOSS ACCOUNT contains several adjustments compared with an historical cost one. There is a DEPRECIATION adjustment to reflect the fact that depreciation based on a current cost would be higher (when prices of the assets are rising), and a COST OF SALES ADJUSTMENT to recognise the effect of changing prices on STOCKS (INVENTORIES). However, the most controversial adjustments in CCA systems are for monetary items. In SSAP 16 there was a MONETARY WORKING CAPITAL ADJUSTMENT to take account of the effect of price changes on DEBTORS and CREDITORS; and a GEARING ADJUSTMENT which is an adjustment connected with the fact that a business gains at the expense of lenders when the value of money falls because of rising prices.

CURRENT LIABILITIES

Those amounts on a BALANCE SHEET that are expected to be paid by the business within a year. They will include TRADE CREDITORS (accounts payable), certain tax LIABILITIES, and proposed DIVIDENDS. Bank overdrafts are included on the grounds that they fluctuate in size and are technically recallable at short notice.

If you owe your bank a hundred pounds, you have a problem, but if you owe it a million it has.
John Maynard Keynes (1883–1946) in *The Economist,*
February 13th 1982, p. 11

CURRENT PURCHASING POWER ACCOUNTING

A method of adjusting HISTORICAL COST ACCOUNTING financial statements to take account of inflation. Current purchasing power accounting (CPP) is a UK term.

CURRENT RATIO

The relationship between the CURRENT ASSETS and the CURRENT LIABILITIES of a business. It is a measure of LIQUIDITY that can be used when comparing one COMPANY with another or one year with another. A higher ratio means greater liquidity and a greater probability that CREDITORS can be paid. However, it may mean that the resources of the business are inefficiently tied up in unproductive ASSETS such as cash or DEBTORS. An even more short-run test of liquidity is to calculate the QUICK RATIO or acid test. This omits the less current assets such as STOCKS (INVENTORIES).

CURRENT REPLACEMENT COST

The amount that would have to be paid to replace an asset at any moment, including the cost of purchase. A problem that will often arise is that an exact replacement is no longer available. The replacement cost of a "modern equivalent asset" will then have to be used, adjusting for differences in the services provided. In practice, the current replacement cost (CRC) is often estimated by applying price indices for the particular asset to its original cost.

CURRENT VALUE ACCOUNTING

A particular version of price-change adjusted accounting. The main adjustments (from HISTORICAL COST ACCOUNTING) of current value accounting are for the price changes of the business's ASSETS, not for general inflation (see INFLATION ACCOUNTING).

Day books

Part of the DOUBLE ENTRY book-keeping system. They are the books of account which initially record the frequent transactions of a business, such as SALES and purchases, so that the main accounting records are not swamped with masses of detail. Thus there may be a sales day book, a purchases day book, and so on. These books of original entry are totalled periodically, perhaps daily, and the totals taken to the main ACCOUNTS.

> *He's an articled clerk. He seems to know his job. He can't get over the way our accounts are kept. He told me he never expected a theatre to be run on such business-like lines. He says the way some of those firms in the City keep their accounts is enough to turn your hair grey.*
> W. Somerset Maugham (1874–1965), *Theatre*, 1937, ch. 1

DCF

See DISCOUNTED CASH FLOW.

Debentures

Certain types of loans, usually long-term, made to a COMPANY. Normally debentures are "secured" on the ASSETS of the company by mortgage deeds. Thus a debenture-holder would be able to persuade a court to force a company to sell these assets if the company was otherwise unable to meet the terms of the loan.

Debit

The word debit is naturally associated with DOUBLE ENTRY, but predates it. It derives from the Latin for "he owes". Thus when a merchant's only records were of the amounts owed to him and by him, the debit was one of the two types of record. An entry in the accounting records saying "Smith debit 100" merely records that Smith owes 100, perhaps for a sale to Smith without immediate receipt of cash.

In the full double-entry system, all increases in ASSETS and EXPENSES and all decreases in CAPITAL, LIABILITIES or REVENUES are debits. If the recording has been done correctly, the total of the debits will always equal the total of the credits.

The debits are to be found on the left-hand side of ACCOUNTS. This has always been the case, and may be because the left (*sinister* in Latin) is regarded as "bad" (this was the side of Judas at the Last Supper, of the goats at the Last Judgment, and so on). The "bad" people who have not paid the business yet are shown on the left. The "good" people who extend CREDIT to the business are shown on the right.

DEBTORS

By derivation "debitors", that is those with DEBIT balances in the BOOKS of account of a business. Debit, as explained in the preceding entry, means "he owes". In a BALANCE SHEET debtors are usually mostly TRADE DEBTORS, that is customers who have not yet paid cash. Such amounts are shown as CURRENT ASSETS because they are not intended for continuing use in the business. The debtors are valued at what they are expected to pay, bearing in mind the principle of CONSERVATISM. Thus BAD DEBTS are written off and provisions are made for debts that may not be collectable. The provisions may be either specific (against particular suspect debts) or general (based on the average experience of bad debts).

Creditors have no real affection for their debtors, but only a desire that they may be preserved that they may repay.

Aristotle (384–322 BC), *Nicomachean Ethics*, bk. IX, ch. 7

DEFERRED CREDIT

An amount recognised in the financial statements but not yet treated as a realised gain in the PROFIT AND LOSS ACCOUNT. The deferred CREDIT or INCOME is stored as a credit balance on the BALANCE SHEET while waiting to be treated as income.

DEFERRED INCOME

See DEFERRED CREDIT.

DEFERRED TAX

Caused by TIMING DIFFERENCES between when an amount is recognised for accounting INCOME purposes and when it is recognised for TAXABLE INCOME. For example, suppose that DEPRECIATION for tax purposes (that is CAPITAL ALLOWANCES) is more rapid than for accounting purposes. In that case, in the early years of an asset's life tax depreciation will be larger than accounting depreciation (and vice versa later). Thus there are timing differences. In order to account fully for deferred tax, an additional deferred tax charge would be recorded to represent tax at current rates on the excess of the tax allowance over the accounting charge for depreciation. A deferred tax liability would also be recorded in this amount. In the UK, deferred tax assets and liabilities are accounted for only when they are expected to crystallise in the foreseeable future. In the United States the rules require accounting for TEMPORARY DIFFERENCES rather than for timing differences.

He's spending a year dead for tax reasons.
Douglas Adams, *The Restaurant at the End of the Universe*, 1980, p. 89

DEPRECIATION

A charge against the PROFIT of a period to represent the wearing out of FIXED ASSETS in that period. So machinery and equipment, vehicles and buildings are depreciated, and land normally is not. The technique of depreciation means that accountants do not charge the whole cost of a fixed asset against the profit of the year of purchase, but charge it gradually over the years of its use and wearing out. This fits with the MATCHING concept. The word AMORTISATION is also used, particularly in the context of INTANGIBLE ASSETS.

DEPRIVAL VALUE

The amount by which a business would be worse off if it were deprived of a particular asset. This is sometimes referred to as its value to the business or value to the owner. When trying to arrive at a realistic and current value of individual ASSETS in order to present a BALANCE SHEET, this method has much to commend it. It should be said at once, however, that deprival value is not the conventional valuation method for financial statements; HISTORICAL COST ACCOUNTING is used instead.

Nevertheless, in the UK, Australia and New Zealand, deprival value has been a method used for supplementary financial statements designed to take the changing prices of assets into account; for example, as required for listed and large UK companies by SSAP 16 of 1980–85.

The deprival value of an asset depends upon the intentions of the business that owns it. If an asset would be replaced, its deprival value is its net CURRENT REPLACEMENT COST (CRC); this would be the normal case. However, for assets that would not be replaced, the deprival value would be the NET REALISABLE VALUE (NRV) if the asset was about to be sold, or ECONOMIC VALUE if it was to continue in use. An example of the latter would be an obsolete, but still used, cotton mill. It still produces worthwhile goods; it will perhaps not be replaced at all; but it is not to be sold (except for scrap when it falls to pieces). In that case the NRV might be very low and would not be relevant, and the CRC would be unrealistically high. Thus the amount recoverable from its future use is what would be lost if the asset were lost.

DEVELOPMENT EXPENDITURE
See RESEARCH AND DEVELOPMENT.

DIRECT COSTS
Those costs which can be associated with the production of particular units or types of products, such as manufacturing wages or manufacturing materials.

DIRECTIVE
A blueprint for a law that must be enacted throughout the European Union. The European Commission is keen to promote the ideal of the

"common market" by trying to remove the barriers to the movement of goods and services, people and CAPITAL. Part of this effort is the HARMONISATION of COMPANY LAW and accounting, through the drafting and adoption of Directives, which have to be enacted in all member states. The commission cannot adopt a Directive; that has to be done by the Council of Ministers, on which each member state is represented.

DIRECTORS' REPORT

Part of the contents of the ANNUAL REPORT of a UK COMPANY. By law it must contain such detailed disclosures as directors' shareholdings, and so on; charitable and political donations; a review of the past year and discussion of future plans; and many other matters. The Directors' Report must be examined by the company's auditors to ensure that it is "consistent with" the financial statements.

In the United States there is no direct equivalent. However, similar information is to be found in Form 10-K which SEC-registered companies must prepare (see SECURITIES AND EXCHANGE COMMISSION).

DISCONTINUED/DISCONTINUING OPERATIONS

Operations whose INCOME, ASSETS or CASH FLOW may need to be separately disclosed in order to enable prediction of the figures for continuing operations.

DISCOUNTED CASH FLOW

Future CASH FLOW, adjusted to take account of its timing. Discounted cash flows are used when making investment choices between competing projects. The most reliable method of deciding which project is best and whether any particular one is worth doing is to work out each project's NET PRESENT VALUE (NPV) by adding up all the discounted expected net cash flows. The NPV calculation will include the outflow of the initial investment. A project with a positive NPV is worth doing; the project with the highest NPV is the best.

DISCOUNT RATE

Either the relevant rate for discounting future inflows or outflows of cash, for a particular person or business (see DISCOUNTED CASH FLOW); or the rate at which discount houses or other banks can borrow from the central bank.

DISTRIBUTABLE PROFITS AND RESERVES

In general the profits of this year, plus previous years' undistributed profits, which are legally available for payment as DIVIDENDS. Of course, whether they are so distributed will depend upon the COMPANY's need for investment funds, its available cash resources, and so on.

In the UK there is an apparently simple definition for all companies: accumulated realised profits less accumulated realised losses (see REALISED PROFITS). The law makes it clear that this is to be interpreted in the context of strict HISTORICAL COST ACCOUNTING. If, for example, any FIXED ASSETS have been revalued, with subsequent extra DEPRECIATION charges, the legally distributable PROFIT will be different from that in the BALANCE SHEET. For a PUBLIC COMPANY there is a slightly more restrictive definition, based on the sufficiency of NET ASSETS compared with distributable profits.

In the United States, depending on the state in which a company is incorporated, the legally distributable profits (unrestricted earnings) will depend upon an earned surplus or a net assets rule (or both) similar to those above.

DIVIDENDS

The return to shareholders, the owners of companies. Unlike INTEREST, which is a return to lenders, dividends do not have to be paid. They can be forgone for many years if the COMPANY deems this suitable for LIQUIDITY, expansion, tax saving or other reasons. Furthermore, dividends are not at a fixed percentage, except for PREFERENCE SHARES. If a company does well, the shareholders probably benefit by higher dividends, sooner or later. Dividends, being a return to the owners, or an appropriation rather than an expense, are not charged in the calculation of PROFIT, nor are they tax deductible for the paying company.

DIVIDEND COVER

The number of times that the most recent annual dividend could have been paid out of the most recent PROFIT. It gives an indication of how secure the future dividend payments are; a high cover suggests room for CONTINGENCIES.

DIVIDEND YIELD

The most recent total annual dividend per share (grossed up with the tax CREDIT) divided by the market price. This is an indication of the cash return that can be expected by buying a particular share. However, it should be borne in mind that the shareholders also benefit from undistributed profits, since these increase the value of their COMPANY and will lead to future DIVIDENDS or capital gains.

What advantages a merchant derives from double entry book-keeping! It is among the finest inventions of the human mind; and every good householder should introduce it into his economy.
Johann Wolfgang von Goethe (1749–1832),
Wilhelm Meister's Apprenticeship, 1795–6, 1, x

DOUBLE ENTRY

A system of BOOK-KEEPING that records two aspects of every transaction. It is an Italian invention that gradually became fully developed in the northern city states in the 14th century, probably in response to substantial increases in the complexity of business, particularly the extensive trading on credit, foreign branches and JOINT VENTURE trading. Systems of single entry had been used for millennia. They involved the recording of cash amounts, and of debts to and from persons outside the business. An entry of DEBIT meant "he owes", and an entry of CREDIT meant "he trusts" (that is, we owe him). Gradually it became clear that every transaction could be seen to have two effects that might both be recorded by a debit and a credit each time. For example, the creation of an asset (a debit) might be the result of INCOME (a credit) or the reduction of another asset.

The system has been expanded to include all possible transactions. This enables the complete recording of SALES, cash, purchases, debts, various categories of EXPENSES, and so on. Each type of transaction is recorded on a separate account. Each account has debits on the left and credits on the right. If the book-keeping has been done correctly, at the end of the period the total debits in the system will equal the total credits. The system is self-balancing and makes the search for errors easier. Further, a balance can be struck on an account at any time, in order to see, for example, how much cash should be present, how much any debtor owes, or how many sales there have been.

For very numerous types of transactions, such as sales, there are usually books of original entry (for example, sales DAY BOOKS or a JOURNAL) that record the daily transactions, and put a summary through to the main double-entry records.

At the end of an accounting period a TRIAL BALANCE is prepared. This is a listing of all the balances on the ACCOUNTS (having netted off debits against credits in each particular account). This should show equality of the total debits and total credits. The balances can then be used to prepare the financial statements. The balances for REVENUES and expenses are put to a PROFIT AND LOSS ACCOUNT (INCOME STATEMENT); the balances for ASSETS, LIABILITIES and CAPITAL go to the BALANCE SHEET.

The system of book-keeping by double entry is, perhaps, the most beautiful one in the wide domain of literature or science. Were it less common, it would be the admiration of the learned world.
Edwin T. Freedley (1827–1904), *Practical Treatise on Business*, 1853, ch. VI

EARNINGS

A technical accounting term meaning the amount of PROFIT (normally for a year) available to the ordinary shareholders. That is, it is the profit after all operating EXPENSES, INTEREST charges, taxes and DIVIDENDS on PREFERENCE SHARES. In the UK earnings includes EXTRAORDINARY ITEMS. However, investment analysts and the *Financial Times* use an alternative calculation called "headline earnings" which excludes various expenses and REVENUES in order to estimate the sustainable profit for shareholders.

EARNINGS PER SHARE

Exactly what its name suggests: earnings per share (EPS) is the most recent year's total EARNINGS divided by the number of ORDINARY SHARES.

EARNINGS YIELD

The EARNINGS PER SHARE divided by the market price. The reciprocal of this is the PRICE/EARNINGS RATIO. Such a figure will indicate the return that might be expected from an investment in the share, and will be an index of its popularity.

ECONOMIC CONSEQUENCES

The possible real economic effects of particular accounting rules. Consideration of these is a relatively recent development in the setting of ACCOUNTING STANDARDS, so far mainly in the United States, and mainly by commentators rather than by standard-setters.

> *There are few subjects, other than economics, that have succeeded in being simultaneously denounced by both academics and practitioners. Accounting has attained that pinnacle.*
> Colin Mayer, "The Real Value of Company Accounts", *Fiscal Studies*, vol. 9, no. 1, February 1988

ECONOMIC VALUE

A way of valuing ASSETS at the expected future net cash flows from them, discounted to the present.

The "discounting" is designed to adjust for the fact that present money is more valuable than the same nominal amount of future money (see DISCOUNTED CASH FLOW).

There can be little doubt that this is in some sense "correct" but, like many of the concepts of economics, it is strong on theory but weak on practicality. As a general basis for valuing assets in a BALANCE SHEET it is a non-starter; the problem being that values reported to outsiders (such as shareholders) need to be reliable, objective and auditable. The economic value of an asset rests upon the prediction of all the future cash flows coming from it, and upon an estimation of the appropriate DISCOUNT RATE. This is far too subjective for financial reporting purposes, although it does appear as part of the DEPRIVAL VALUE concept used in special cases, and often without discounting in systems of CURRENT COST ACCOUNTING.

A further problem with economic value is that it will probably be practically impossible to estimate the CASH FLOW from any particular asset, since groups of assets work together to produce products and cash flows. The value of the output of a machine depends upon other machines around it, and upon the factory that it works in.

However, for internal investment appraisal purposes, when dealing with the future and with subjectivity, economic value or NET PRESENT VALUE is very useful.

If all economists were laid end to end, they would not reach a conclusion.

Gerorge Bernard Shaw (1856–1950), attributed

EFFICIENT MARKET HYPOTHESIS

An elegant and important theory, usually applied to the price of SHARES on large stock exchanges, that all publicly available information is immediately taken into account in the price of shares. In markets such as the New York or London stock exchanges there are many buyers and sellers of shares, the prices are well known, and much other information is freely available. So any new relevant information about a COMPANY would be expected rapidly to affect its price.

There is considerable evidence, especially from the United States, that large stock exchanges are fairly efficient markets in the above sense. However, few companies, investors, brokers, and so on behave as if they are. Of course, the efficiency of the market depends upon buyers and sellers behaving as if it were not efficient. Efficiency depends upon all the analysis being done and the information being produced.

EMPLOYEE REPORTING

Telling the employees how the COMPANY is performing, with the aid of a specially designed ANNUAL REPORT. This has become more common recently, particularly in the UK, probably because of a general recognition that employees should be more informed and involved in companies.

ENTITY CONVENTION

The entity convention is to view the business as separate from its owners. This is standard for accounting and, for many businesses, it is also the legal position. It enables accountants to prepare balance sheets that balance, because amounts contributed by and earned for the owners can be shown as CAPITAL, with the LIABILITIES owed to non-owners.

The entity view is an extension of this, and can be contrasted to the PROPRIETARY VIEW. The entity view would see the business's viewpoint; the proprietary view sees things from the point of view of the shareholders in the parent company.

ENTITY VIEW

See ENTITY CONVENTION.

EPS

See EARNINGS PER SHARE.

EQUITY

A word with several shades of meaning in different countries. In general, it refers to the proprietor's share in a business. In the United States, it is a common abbreviation for STOCKHOLDERS' EQUITY.

EQUITY METHOD
See ASSOCIATED COMPANY.

EQUITY SHARES
A UK expression for SHARES that are not redeemable and do not have any restricting characteristics, such as limited rights to DIVIDENDS.

EXCEPTIONAL ITEMS
A UK expression for those items in a PROFIT AND LOSS ACCOUNT that are within the ordinary activities of the business, but are of unusual size. The treatment for these, as laid down in ACCOUNTING STANDARDS (FRS 3), is to disclose them separately in the profit and loss account or the notes to it. Such items are to be distinguished from EXTRAORDINARY ITEMS.

EX DIVIDEND
A share is ex dividend (ex div) if sales of it would not entitle the purchaser to the forthcoming dividend. So if you buy a share in the period leading up to a dividend payment it will usually be ex div. For most of the time a share is the opposite of this, namely CUM DIVIDEND.

EXPENSES
When used by accountants this is a technical term. It means all those payments, whenever physically made, that relate to the period in question. For example, a business may pay its electricity account after the end of the year in which the electricity was used; or it may pay its rent in advance. Such amounts are ACCRUED EXPENSES and PREPAYMENTS, respectively. Accountants would treat both as expenses of the year to which they relate, showing the accruals or prepayments in a BALANCE SHEET.

This practice is part of the MATCHING or accruals concept. It is designed to lead to a fairer presentation of PROFIT for a period. Profit is calculated by taking the expenses from the REVENUES of the period.

EXPERT COMPTABLE

The nearest equivalent in France to a professionally qualified accountant in the Anglo-American sense. Most *experts comptables* are auditors of French companies. The Ordre des Experts Comptables is a self-regulating professional body. However, most of the rules for accounting come from government-controlled institutions, and there is also a government-controlled AUDITING body to which many *experts comptables* belong.

EXPOSURE DRAFTS

Documents that precede the issue of ACCOUNTING STANDARDS. They are intended to attract a response from companies, auditors, academics, investment analysts, financial institutions, and so on.

EXTRAORDINARY GENERAL MEETING

An extraordinary general meeting (EGM), as its name suggests, does not happen very often to any particular COMPANY. It will be held, within the rules laid down by COMPANY LAW and the company's own ARTICLES OF ASSOCIATION (BYLAWS), when certain unusual events require it. For example, a certain proportion of the shareholders may demand an EGM in order to question their directors on alleged improprieties or to deal with a takeover. An EGM may also be held when the company has SOLVENCY problems. Normally, the shareholders will only meet at the ANNUAL GENERAL MEETING.

EXTRAORDINARY ITEMS

Gains or losses which are outside the ordinary activities of the business, are of material size, and are not expected to recur. In the UK the definition of "ordinary" in FRS 3 is so wide that the recognition of an extraordinary item is unlikely. However, in some other countries the definition is wider, and could include such items as gains on the sale of FIXED ASSETS.

FACTORING

An expression particularly associated with DEBTORS. Factoring such debts means selling them to a financial institution in return for a proportion of the face value. This is a technique similar to borrowing. The discount will be designed to include an implied rate of INTEREST, the costs of collection and the possibility of default.

FAIR PRESENTATION

Financial statements in the United States that are fully audited and prepared in accordance with GENERALLY ACCEPTED ACCOUNTING PRINCIPLES (GAAP) are required to "present fairly" the position and results of a COMPANY. To a large extent this means obeying the GAAP rules, but the concept of fairness may transcend that, to include an assessment of the overall picture given by the financial statements. A connected doctrine is that financial statements should reflect SUBSTANCE OVER FORM.

FAIR VALUE

A technical accounting term which generally means, in the case of an asset, its CURRENT REPLACEMENT COST. In a BUSINESS COMBINATION accounted for as an ACQUISITION, the ASSETS and LIABILITIES of the new SUBSIDIARY are brought into the CONSOLIDATED FINANCIAL STATEMENTS at fair values, not their previous book values.

FASB

See FINANCIAL ACCOUNTING STANDARDS BOARD.

FÉDÉRATION DES EXPERTS COMPTABLES EUROPÉENS

A European body of accountants which began work in 1987, although it had predecessor bodies. One of its committees specialises in advising the European Commission on the HARMONISATION of COMPANY LAW.

FIFO

See FIRST IN, FIRST OUT.

FII
See FRANKED INVESTMENT INCOME.

FINANCE ACTS
The UK name for the annual laws that introduce tax changes and the new rates of tax. They follow Finance Bills, which themselves follow Budget Statements by the Chancellor of the Exchequer.

FINANCE LEASE
A LEASE which is treated by accountants as though the lessee had borrowed money and bought the leased ASSETS. That is, the lease is capitalised. Generally, such leases are those taken out for a large proportion of the life of the asset. The lessor treats the lease contract as a receivable. Leases that are not capitalised are called operating leases.

FINANCIAL ACCOUNTING
A fairly vague term which covers BOOK-KEEPING and the subsequent processing and analysis that leads to the preparation of financial statements for shareholders and others. It may be contrasted, for example, with MANAGEMENT ACCOUNTING, which deals with the use of accounting data by managers inside a business to enable better planning and control.

FINANCIAL ACCOUNTING STANDARDS BOARD
A body set up in the United States in 1973 to set ACCOUNTING STANDARDS on measurement, valuation and disclosure practices to be followed in the preparation of financial statements. In this task it is given "substantial authoritative support" by a government body, the SECURITIES AND EXCHANGE COMMISSION (SEC). US companies that want their securities to be publicly traded must be registered and file financial statements with the SEC, which will not accept those that disobey Financial Accounting Standards Board (FASB) standards. Thus the standards have considerable power for the minority of US companies that are SEC registered.

The FASB has seven full-time board members and a substantial research staff. The board members are appointed by the independent Financial Accounting Foundation, which also raises the money for the FASB. The donations come from companies and accounting firms, presumably fearing the intervention of the SEC if no private body were capable of setting standards. Donations are limited for any one donor, in order to preserve independence.

The FASB works by due process, which includes prior research, wide circulation of EXPOSURE DRAFTS and public hearings before a standard is issued.

FINANCIAL INSTRUMENT

A contract which gives rise to a financial asset of one enterprise and a financial liability or EQUITY instrument of another. Since cash is a financial asset, this definition is very wide, including simple loans as well as much more complex financial arrangements such as convertible DEBENTURES and derivatives.

FINANCIAL REPORTING REVIEW PANEL

See REVIEW PANEL.

FINANCIAL REPORTING STANDARD

An accounting standard as promulgated in the UK by the ACCOUNTING STANDARDS BOARD since 1990. Its commonly used acronym is FRS.

FINANCIAL YEAR

The usual UK expression for the period for which the ANNUAL REPORT and ACCOUNTS are prepared. The most popular dates for the year end are December 31 and March 31, which coincides with the tax year for companies. Some companies account for exactly 52 or 53 weeks, so their precise year end may vary by a day or two in each year. In the United States the analogous expression is FISCAL YEAR.

FIRST IN, FIRST OUT

A common assumption for accounting purposes about the flow of items of raw materials or other STOCKS (INVENTORIES), generally known by its acronym FIFO. It need not be expected to correspond with physical reality, but may be made for accounting purposes. The assumption is that the first units to be received as part of stocks are the first ones to be used up or sold. This means that the most recent units are deemed to be those left at the period end. When prices are rising, and assuming a reasonably constant purchasing of materials, FIFO leads to a fairly up-to-date closing stock figure. However, it gives an out-of-date and therefore low figure for the COST OF SALES. This leads to what many argue is an overstatement of PROFIT figures when prices are rising.

FISCAL YEAR

The US expression for the period for which companies prepare their annual financial statements. The majority of US companies use December 31 as the fiscal year end, which corresponds with the year end for tax purposes. As an accounting term it is a slight misnomer because fiscal year really means tax year, and it is by no means for all companies that the accounting year and the tax year both terminate on December 31. The equivalent UK term is FINANCIAL YEAR.

FIXED ASSETS

Mainly a UK rather than a US expression, meaning the ASSETS that are to continue to be used in the business, such as land, buildings and machines. The opposite are CURRENT ASSETS, such as cash or STOCKS (INVENTORIES). The Companies Act defines fixed assets as those "intended for use on a continuing basis". The equivalent US expression is usually "property, plant and equipment".

It is normal for fixed assets to wear out through use or the passing of time, in other words they have limited useful lives. This is recognised by a charge against PROFIT and a reduction in the holding value of the assets called DEPRECIATION. Some fixed assets may not wear out, such as plots of land. It could well be that the owners of Westminster Abbey, for example, might feel that its useful life is so long that depreciation is not a practical concept.

FIXED COSTS

The costs of a business that cannot be altered in the short term, such as factory rents or staff on contracts. Fixed costs will normally be OVERHEADS that relate to several product lines or jobs. For example, the chief executive's salary and the INTEREST on loans will be fixed overhead costs.

FOREIGN CURRENCY TRANSLATION

The "translation" of the financial statements of a foreign SUBSIDIARY or branch into the currency of the parent COMPANY to enable the preparation of CONSOLIDATED FINANCIAL STATEMENTS. Translation is now distinguished from currency conversion in that the latter involves the physical exchange of money from one currency to another. Translation is purely an accounting exercise, but it is a complex and controversial one.

FORM 20-F

A document required to be filed annually with the SECURITIES AND EXCHANGE COMMISSION by those non-US registrants who do not produce an ANNUAL REPORT based on US rules.

FRANKED INVESTMENT INCOME

DIVIDENDS received by one UK COMPANY from another. These are not chargeable to CORPORATION TAX because they have already borne corporation tax in the paying company. Such INCOME is called franked investment income (FII) because it has been franked, that is taxed or stamped. The receipt of FII by a company reduces the amount of corporation tax that has to be paid in advance as a result of its payments of dividends (see ADVANCE CORPORATION TAX).

FRS

See FINANCIAL REPORTING STANDARD.

FUNDS FLOW STATEMENTS

See SOURCE AND APPLICATION OF FUNDS.

GAAP
See GENERALLY ACCEPTED ACCOUNTING PRINCIPLES.

GAAS
See GENERALLY ACCEPTED AUDITING STANDARDS.

GASB
See GOVERNMENTAL ACCOUNTING STANDARDS BOARD.

GEARING
A measurement of the degree to which a business is funded by loans rather than shareholders' EQUITY. The US expression is leverage. Different analysts of a COMPANY's financial position will use different definitions of gearing. The main rule, as with other RATIOS, is to try to be consistent from year to year or company to company. Common measures of gearing are long-term loans:total CAPITAL, or long-term loans:shareholders' equity. The higher the proportion of loan finance, the higher is the gearing.

A further measure of the danger of INSOLVENCY is INTEREST gearing, which measures the extent to which a company's pre-tax, pre-interest PROFIT is pre-empted by the need to pay interest. Higher interest gearing means greater danger.

GEARING ADJUSTMENT
One of the several adjustments to PROFIT, to be found in some systems of CURRENT COST ACCOUNTING, that take account of changing prices. The other main adjustments are DEPRECIATION and the COST OF SALES ADJUSTMENT, which are extra charges against profit when prices are rising. The gearing adjustment is designed to take account of the degree to which these deductions in a particular COMPANY are compensated for by the fact that it is financed by loans (that is, the degree to which it has high GEARING).

GENERALLY ACCEPTED ACCOUNTING PRINCIPLES
A technical term, particularly used in the United States where it would include the ACCOUNTING STANDARDS of the FINANCIAL ACCOUNTING STANDARDS

BOARD and extant rules of predecessor bodies. Also included are some of the rules propounded by the SECURITIES AND EXCHANGE COMMISSION (SEC) as Accounting Series Releases and Financial Reporting Releases. The SEC requires that companies registered with it prepare audited financial statements according to US generally accepted accounting principles (GAAP).

GENERALLY ACCEPTED AUDITING STANDARDS

A technical term, used in the US, to include those rules that should be followed by auditors when carrying out a full audit on financial statements, particularly for SECURITIES AND EXCHANGE COMMISSION filing purposes. Its acronym is GAAS.

GESELLSCHAFT MIT BESCHRÄNKTER HAFTUNG

The abbreviation for a German or Swiss private limited company. A *Gesellschaft mit beschränkter Haftung* (GmbH) is not the exact equivalent of a UK private company or a US non-registered company, and is a little like a PARTNERSHIP in its ownership STOCK.

GILT-EDGED SECURITIES

A UK expression for some loans made to the government. So secure are the INTEREST payments and eventual repayment deemed to be, that this form of loan STOCK is seen to be almost risk-free or "as good as gold", hence gilt-edged. Another name for certain types of government securities is Treasury bills. This opens the door to the possibility of extreme confusion for UK accountants and businessmen when they meet the expression TREASURY STOCK in US balance sheets. In the US treasury stock means a COMPANY's own SHARES bought back by the company and held in the corporate treasury. The UK expression for this is OWN SHARES.

GMBH

See *GESELLSCHAFT MIT BESCHRÄNKTER HAFTUNG*.

GOING CONCERN

An important underlying concept in accounting

practice. The assumption for most businesses is that they will continue for the foreseeable future. This means that, for most purposes, the break-up or forced-sale value of the ASSETS is not relevant. Particularly for FIXED ASSETS, what they could be sold for may be a severe underestimate of their value to a business in terms of REPLACEMENT COST or ECONOMIC VALUE. Their NET REALISABLE VALUE is therefore ignored in most systems of accounting, including the conventional system, HISTORICAL COST ACCOUNTING.

Companies do not need to disclose that they are following the going concern convention. However, if there are doubts that a business is a going concern, the convention should be abandoned in order to show realisable values, where appropriate.

GOODWILL

The amount paid for a business in excess of the FAIR VALUE of its ASSETS at the date of ACQUISITION. It exists because a GOING CONCERN business is usually worth more than the sum of the values of its separable NET ASSETS. This may be looked upon as its ability to earn future profits above those of a similar newly formed COMPANY, or it may be seen as the loyalty of customers, the established network of contacts, trained staff and skilled management.

If the business being bought is unincorporated (such as a PARTNERSHIP) it will be absorbed into the legal and accounting entity of the acquiring company. Any resulting purchased goodwill could be shown in the BALANCE SHEET of the company. In the more usual cases, where a company is bought, the resulting goodwill in the CONSOLIDATED FINANCIAL STATEMENTS is called goodwill on consolidation. Assets are brought into the consolidated financial statements at their fair value rather than their BOOK VALUE because the former is a better indication of the COST to the group of companies of the newly arrived assets. The exception to this practice is MERGER ACCOUNTING. In the UK the normal practice until 1998 was to write goodwill off against group RESERVES immediately on acquisition. In many other countries goodwill is treated as an asset and is amortised over its life (for example, limited to 40 years in the United States). From 1998 onwards, FRS 10 requires newly purchased goodwill to be treated as an asset (see essay, page 9).

GOVERNMENTAL ACCOUNTING STANDARDS BOARD

A US standard-setting body that represents an extension of the work of the Financial Accounting Foundation which also controls the FINANCIAL ACCOUNTING STANDARDS BOARD. The task of the Governmental Accounting Standards Board (GASB) is to develop accounting standards for government-controlled enterprises.

GROSS PROFIT

For a manufacturing company, gross profit is the difference between the value of its SALES and the COST OF SALES. The latter includes the purchases of raw materials, adjusted for changes to STOCKS (INVENTORIES), and all the other costs of producing the goods that were sold in the period, such as factory wages. Non-manufacturing EXPENSES, such as administration costs and INTEREST charges, are then deducted from the gross profit to arrive at NET PROFIT before tax.

GROUP ACCOUNTS

The financial statements of a group of companies (the parent company and its subsidiaries). The Companies Act requires group accounts to be prepared by groups, and this means CONSOLIDATED FINANCIAL STATEMENTS.

GROUPE D'ETUDES DES EXPERTS COMPTABLES DE LA CEE

The EC Accountants' Study Group was set up at the request of the European Commission. Its task was to respond to the commission on matters concerning accountants, particularly draft Directives. Its functions were absorbed into the FÉDÉRATION DES EXPERTS COMPTABLES EUROPÉENS at the end of 1986.

H

HARMONISATION

The making of practices more compatible, though not necessarily exactly standardised. The word is commonly used in the context of the effort of the European Commission and Council of the European Union to bring about compatibility of financial reporting and COMPANY LAW. The key to this, of course, is enforceability. This is achieved primarily by passing Directives on company law, which have to be enacted and enforced by member states.

Harmony would lose its attractiveness if it did not have a background of discord.
Tehyi Hsieh, *Chinese Epigrams Inside Out and Proverbs*, 1948

HEADLINE EARNINGS

A measure of a COMPANY'S EARNINGS as calculated by a formula set out in the UK by the Institute of Investment Management and Research. This is the definition of earnings used by many analysts and newspapers. It removes from the earnings calculation certain items deemed to be non-recurring or non-operating, such as gains on the sale of FIXED ASSETS.

HISTORICAL COST ACCOUNTING

The conventional system of accounting, widely established throughout the world, except in some countries where inflation is endemic and high. Even in these cases historical cost records are maintained and subjected to simple indexation adjustments for the preparation of financial statements.

Under historical cost accounting the purchases of ASSETS, such as land, buildings, machines and STOCKS (INVENTORIES), are recorded at their purchase price at the date of acquisition. Generally that value is not subsequently changed except to write down the value below COST in order to recognise any loss in value or normal wearing out. The latter is known as DEPRECIATION. Other balances, such as DEBTORS or various sorts of LIABIL-

ITIES, are valued at what is expected to be received or paid in cash.

HOLDING COMPANY

A COMPANY that owns or controls others. In the narrow use of the expression, it implies that the company does not actively trade but operates through various subsidiaries. The accounting treatment for such parent–SUBSIDIARY relationships is to prepare CONSOLIDATED FINANCIAL STATEMENTS for the combined group.

HOLDING GAINS

During periods of rising prices the NET REALISABLE VALUE of ASSETS will rise. When these assets are sold, part or all of the gain realised is not a result of the normal trading operations of the business but is a holding gain. Holding gains may, of course, also be unrealised but realisable, up to the point of sale of the asset concerned. Conventional HISTORICAL COST ACCOUNTING ignores realisable holding gains and records only the realised gains. Thus profits are distorted, particularly in the year of sale of significant assets. Most systems of INFLATION ACCOUNTING either deduct or separately identify some version of holding gains, in order to calculate OPERATING PROFIT.

HUMAN ASSETS

It is clear that the total value of some businesses rests heavily on their human assets, such as loyal staff and skilled managers. At one extreme, the value of owning a football or basketball team may rest almost entirely on human assets. In conventional accounting, such ASSETS have been ignored because of the difficulty of establishing an objective and auditable value. The future ECONOMIC VALUE of employees is obviously hard to determine with any accuracy. Even using HISTORICAL COST ACCOUNTING, it would not be clear exactly what was spent on creating the assets, nor how much of what was spent was wasted.

Nevertheless, some schemes for the valuation of human assets have been worked out. They involve the accumulation of such costs as recruitment and training, with a reduction for staff who have left. Practical application has not followed these theoretical exercises, so human assets remain a part of the mysterious total of GOODWILL.

> *The value of a man can only be measured with regard to other men.*
> Nietzsche, *The Will to Power*, 1888

IASC
See INTERNATIONAL ACCOUNTING STANDARDS COMMITTEE.

IFAC
See INTERNATIONAL FEDERATION OF ACCOUNTANTS.

IMPAIRMENT
The loss in value of a fixed asset which is measured by comparing its CARRYING VALUE with its FAIR VALUE or RECOVERABLE AMOUNT. Such a loss would be charged against INCOME.

INCOME
The words REVENUE, PROFIT, EARNINGS and income are used somewhat vaguely by some accountants and business people, and usage in the UK and the United States is slightly different.

In the UK income is not generally used in connection with commercial businesses. Instead there are SALES REVENUES, GROSS PROFIT and NET PROFIT and earnings (in increasing order of the extraction of EXPENSES). The word "income" is associated more with NON-PROFIT organisations.

In the United States income is used more widely in a commercial context instead of profit. (See also COMPREHENSIVE INCOME.)

We ought to define a man's income as the maximum value which he can consume during a week, and still expect to be as well off at the end of the week as he was at the beginning.
J.R. Hicks, *Value and Capital*, 2nd ed., 1946, pt. III, ch. XIV

INCOME AND EXPENDITURE ACCOUNT
A version of the PROFIT AND LOSS ACCOUNT for NON-PROFIT organisations. It retains the MATCHING concept and so includes REVENUES and EXPENSES which relate to the period. (The alternative, RECEIPTS AND PAYMENTS ACCOUNT, concentrates on cash movements instead.) Thus the income and expenditure account for a period shows the surplus or deficit for that period.

INCOME SMOOTHING

Reducing the variation in yearly PROFIT figures; a practice that is not generally acceptable in the UK or the United States. This can be done by charging high PROVISIONS for DEPRECIATION, risks or CONTINGENCIES in successful years, and by reversing or reducing such provisions in poor years. In some countries these provision "slush funds" can be so enormous that the real results of individual years are quite hidden in the final "profit" announcements. Thus someone used to UK or US accounting should take care when reading the financial statements of countries using quite different systems.

INCOME STATEMENT

The US name for the PROFIT AND LOSS ACCOUNT.

INCOME TAX

In the UK unincorporated businesses pay income tax but companies pay CORPORATION TAX. Income tax is calculated by applying a series of stepped, increasing marginal rates to TAXABLE INCOME, which is based on the NET PROFIT for accounting purposes but with some adjustments.

All forms of businesses in the United States pay income tax. It is paid on a quarterly prepayment system, using estimates based on the previous year's profits.

INCOMPLETE RECORDS

These are partial accounting records. The full DOUBLE ENTRY book-keeping system may be found by small or poorly organised businesses to be complex, time-consuming and expensive. Instead, there may be only a cash book, a list of SALES, or records on the backs of envelopes. These can be described by the broad term "incomplete records". Of course, the problem will also occur if the BOOKS are mislaid, stolen or burnt.

Accountants are quite good at taking incomplete records and reconstructing what must have happened, with the aid of bank statements, last year's BALANCE SHEET, and so on. This is necessary to calculate profits for the information of the owner and the tax authorities.

INDIRECT COSTS

The costs of a business that cannot be directly associated with the production of a particular unit or type of product. Examples are machines used for the production of a variety of products at different times of the day; the supervising staff in a factory who look after several product lines; and the heating and rental costs of a manufacturing unit that produces several products.

INFLATION ACCOUNTING

Usually interpreted as encompassing various types of systems that might adjust or replace HISTORICAL COST ACCOUNTING to take account of changing prices. Many such systems are poorly described by the term, because they do not involve a recognition of general price level movements. Systems that do adjust for inflation are called CURRENT PURCHASING POWER ACCOUNTING in the UK or general price level adjusted accounting in the United States.

Alternatives that adjust for the specific price changes affecting the ASSETS and operations of a business are CURRENT COST ACCOUNTING, REPLACEMENT COST ACCOUNTING, and systems that rely on NET REALISABLE VALUE and ECONOMIC VALUE.

In nearly all systems of inflation accounting there are adjustments of BALANCE SHEET assets each year, and also adjustments to PROFIT for DEPRECIATION and COST OF SALES. In some systems there are also adjustments for monetary items, including a GEARING ADJUSTMENT.

In practice, most countries have remained faithful to historical cost for the main financial statements of businesses. However, in some South American countries with very high rates of inflation, general price level adjusted accounting has been adopted. In the Netherlands some companies use replacement cost accounting, and others provide notes on this basis. (For more detail see CURRENT COST ACCOUNTING.)

INSIDER DEALING

The use of information, which is not publicly available, to make decisions about buying or selling publicly traded SHARES.

INSOLVENCY

Generally used to refer to a state in which a business or person is unable to pay debts as they fall due.

A solvent bank is an institution which is able to meet its liabilities as long as nobody desires that it should do so, and which can't meet them at any other time. It is built on the principle that everybody can have his money if he doesn't want it, and not otherwise.

Anonymous, *The Bulletin*, Sydney, c.1893,
in T. Sykes, *Two Centuries of Panic*, 1988, ch. 9

INTANGIBLE ASSETS

ASSETS that are not physical or tangible. Intangible assets that may be shown on a BALANCE SHEET include patents, licences, trade marks and GOODWILL.

The Indian who sold Manhattan for $24.00 was a sharp salesman. If he had put his $24 away at 6% compounded semiannually, it would now be $9.5 billion and he could buy most of the now-improved land back.

S. Branch Walker, *Life*, August 31st 1959

INTEREST

The payment made to lenders as a return on money lent. It may be contrasted to the payments to shareholders, who receive DIVIDENDS. Interest is usually a contractual payment, so an unpaid lender can take legal action against the defaulting borrower. Interest may be paid at a fixed rate or at one that varies with prevailing rates (a floating rate). It is part of the EXPENSES of a business, and is tax deductible.

INTERIM DIVIDEND

It is normal for large UK companies to declare an interim dividend which might be about one-third of the expected dividend for the full year. In the United States quarterly DIVIDENDS are common.

INTERIM REPORT

Generally a half-yearly report by a COMPANY listed on the STOCK EXCHANGE. Such a report must be published, but it need not be audited and is not as detailed as an ANNUAL REPORT. These reports are required to inform shareholders of a company's progress and to allow share prices to adjust more smoothly during the year.

In the United States companies registered with the SECURITIES AND EXCHANGE COMMISSION are required to provide quarterly reports.

INTERNAL AUDIT

The examination of the systems of control and the accuracy of records of a COMPANY by its own staff. This may be distinguished from external AUDITING which involves checking, by or for the owners of resources or companies, on the stewards or managers of those resources. This is called an external audit because it is done by professional accountants who are not day-to-day employees of the company. To some extent internal audit may duplicate or pre-empt the work of external auditors, and may reduce the work and fees of the latter. However, internal audit is also often actively concerned with the discovery and prevention of fraud and with the design and effectiveness of systems of INTERNAL CONTROL.

INTERNAL CHECK

Part of INTERNAL CONTROL, that is office systems designed to make error and fraud difficult. Internal check rests on the separation of duties achieved when two or more employees are involved in control processes. At its simplest, this suggests that at least two people should have to sign or be involved in the completion of cheques or the distribution of cash wages. Good internal check also involves the rotation of duties and insistence on holidays for employees. This ensures that certain elaborate frauds involving the falsification of records cannot be covered up indefinitely.

INTERNAL CONTROL

All those management systems controlling the administration of an organisation. This will include INTERNAL AUDIT, INTERNAL CHECK and a BUDGET. Good internal control will make error and fraud more difficult, and will also make accounting records more reliable.

> *Accounting and control – that is* mainly *what is needed for the "smooth working", for the proper functioning, of the* first phase *of communist society.*
>
> V.I. Lenin (1870–1924), *The State and Revolution*, 1917, ch. 5.4

INTERNAL RATE OF RETURN

The annual percentage PROFITABILITY on the initial investment in a project, taking into account the fact that money received later is worth less than money received earlier. The rate calculated can be compared with the assumed INTEREST cost for the CAPITAL used in the project. The interest cost will depend upon the COMPANY's individual sources and uses of finance. Projects with higher internal rates of return (IRR) will be preferred to those with lower; and all projects carried out should have IRR that exceed the cost of the capital.

The NET PRESENT VALUE method involves similar calculations but is regarded as a more reliable means of discriminating between projects.

INTERNATIONAL ACCOUNTING STANDARDS COMMITTEE

An organisation composed of representatives of over 120 professional accountancy bodies from different countries. The International Accounting Standards Committee (IASC) was formed in 1973 and has its headquarters in London. Its purpose is to devise and promulgate international standards in order to reduce the variation of practices in financial reporting throughout the world. Its member bodies have promised to use their best endeavours to ensure compliance with standards. The standards are generally similar to US and UK practices.

By the late 1990s several countries had begun to base their standards closely on those of the IASC. Negotiations are under way with the IOSCO to make IASC standards acceptable on all the world's stockmarkets for foreign companies.

INTERNATIONAL FEDERATION OF ACCOUNTANTS

A body comprising representatives from the accountancy professions of many nations. The International Federation of Accountants (IFAC) was formed in 1977 and is based in New York. One of its committees sets international AUDITING standards, but it leaves accounting standards to the IASC.

Men with accountancy training occupy positions in business from book-keeper to chairman. All of them will be referred to, often in a derogatory sense, as accountants.

R. Ian Tricker, *The Accountant in Management*, 1967, pt. 1, ch. 1

INTERNATIONAL ORGANIZATION OF SECURITIES COMMISSIONS

An international body of governmental regulators of stock exchanges. Its acronym is IOSCO.

INVENTORIES

The normal US term for raw materials, work-in-progress and goods ready for sale. In the UK the word "STOCKS" is generally used.

INVESTMENT PROPERTY

A property held by a business for investment potential or rental INCOME, rather than for its own occupation. Thus investment properties may be owned by businesses other than property companies. The accounting standard for investment properties (SSAP 19) requires such properties to be revalued annually and not to be subjected to normal DEPRECIATION.

INVESTMENT TRUSTS
Companies whose main purpose is to use the funds contributed by shareholders to own and manage profitably a portfolio of STOCKS and SHARES. Unlike UNIT TRUSTS these are "close-ended funds" in that there are no extra regular contributions from participants. If shareholders wish to extract their funds they must sell their shares to another investor. This would have no direct effect on the trust.

IOSCO
See INTERNATIONAL ORGANIZATION OF SECURITIES COMMISSIONS.

IRR
See INTERNAL RATE OF RETURN.

IRREDEEMABLE DEBENTURES
Securities are irredeemable if there is no provision for their holders to be paid back by the issuing COMPANY. Normally, loans are redeemable but SHARES are not. However, there are exceptions to both these rules; and in the UK there are loans called irredeemable DEBENTURES.

ISSUED SHARE CAPITAL
The amount of share CAPITAL of a COMPANY, at NOMINAL VALUE, that has been issued to the shareholders. Sometimes not all of this has yet been called up. Its MEMORANDUM OF ASSOCIATION specifies the maximum share capital that is authorised for a company, although this can be changed by the shareholders. Often a company will not have issued as many shares as are authorised. The issued capital will be shown in the BALANCE SHEET, and the authorised share capital will be shown in the notes to the financial statements.

All SHARES in the UK, and most shares in the United States, have a NOMINAL VALUE or PAR VALUE.

Normally, shares will be sold by a company at a price above the par value. In the financial statements such shares are recorded "at par" under the heading of share capital, COMMON STOCK, and so on. The excess contributed above the par value is shown as SHARE PREMIUM in the UK or capital surplus/PAID-IN SURPLUS in the United States.

JOINT VENTURE

A co-operative exercise between two or more businesses, often set up for a specific purpose and a limited time.

JOURNAL

A business will usually have many transactions each day. The DOUBLE ENTRY system has to record all these. However, there is a danger that the main BOOKS of account would get swamped with information if each one were recorded separately. Thus for some frequent events, such as SALES, there are special DAY BOOKS. The journal, as its name suggests, is also a day book. It contains a record of the creation of double entries for those types of items that are not sufficiently frequent to have their own specialised day book, such as year-end entries and the correction of errors. Every DEBIT or CREDIT that is recorded will have gone through a day book. Thus all entries can be traced back to their source, where a description and date can be found.

Last in, first out

One of the methods available for the calculation of the COST of STOCKS (INVENTORIES) in those frequent cases where it is difficult or impossible to determine which specific items remain and which have been used. When prices are rising, last in, first out (LIFO) will lead to more up-to-date costs for the inventory used (COST OF SALES) and, thus, lower profits than would be shown by other methods, such as FIFO. It is therefore popular with many companies in the United States, where it is allowed for tax purposes (as long as it is also used in the income statement).

However, the inventory value shown in the BALANCE SHEET may be seriously misleading as it will be based on old prices. The method is therefore discouraged by the appropriate ACCOUNTING STANDARD (SSAP 9) in the UK, and is rarely found. Nevertheless, it is allowed by the Companies Act, although it is not accepted for tax purposes.

Lease

A contract whereby a person or a COMPANY (the lessee) is granted the exclusive right to the use of an asset owned by another (the lessor). In return the lessee makes periodic payments throughout the agreed term of the lease. For a lease that lasts for most of the expected useful life of the asset, the act of leasing is similar to hire purchase, or to a purchase made with a loan from the lessor. In this case, accountants treat the item as an asset and record the future LIABILITIES as if they were loans, despite the fact that the ASSETS are not owned by the lessee. This is an example of the application of the principle of SUBSTANCE OVER FORM. (See also FINANCE LEASE and OPERATING LEASE.)

Ledgers

See BOOKS.

Legal reserves

UNDISTRIBUTABLE RESERVES required to be set up by companies in certain countries for the protection of CREDITORS. In Germany and France, for example, such reserves must be built up to the extent of 10% of ISSUED SHARE CAPITAL. Such reserves are not required in the UK or the United States.

LEVERAGE
The US term for GEARING.

LIABILITIES
Amounts of money that must be paid by a business at some future date. Many liabilities are of known amount and due date of payment. They include long-term loans, bank overdrafts and amounts owed to suppliers. There may be current or non-current liabilities: the former are expected to be paid within a year from the date of the BALANCE SHEET on which they appear. The difference between the CURRENT ASSETS and the CURRENT LIABILITIES is described as NET CURRENT ASSETS.

In some cases amounts that are not quite certain will be included as PROVISIONS for liabilities; they will be valued at the best estimate available. The convention of CONSERVATISM suggests that amounts that are reasonably likely to be liabilities should be treated as such. Less likely amounts are recorded in the notes as CONTINGENCIES.

LIFO
See LAST IN, FIRST OUT.

LIMITED LIABILITY COMPANY
A COMPANY whose owners have limited liability for the debts of their business. The owners of partnerships and sole trader businesses are fully liable in law for the debts of those businesses. Thus the providers of ownership finance for such businesses are usually few in number, and restricted to those who are able and willing to become managers of the business in order to protect their interests.

For really large businesses with thousands of owners another legal form is necessary, so that the owners (or shareholders) may have limited liability for the debts of their business, and therefore be prepared to delegate management to directors. In

1855 in the UK a Companies Act introduced the possibility of registration of companies in limited liability form.

The liability of shareholders is limited to their share CAPITAL. This of course this may damage the interests of lenders. Thus companies are generally not allowed to pay back capital to shareholders, and have to notify lenders of their status by putting after their names such warnings as Ltd, plc (UK) or Ltd, Inc (United States). For equivalent names in some other countries see COMPANY (Table 7).

LIQUIDITY

An expression denoting the cash resources of a business. Thus a COMPANY with ample cash may be said to have good liquidity. Poor liquidity may lead to difficulties in paying debts as they fall due, and to inability to undertake profitable projects due to lack of funds. Of course it may be possible to solve this in the long run by being profitable; or in the short run by selling ASSETS or by issuing more SHARES or long-term loan stock.

One measure of liquidity is the NET CURRENT ASSETS or working capital of a business, which is the CURRENT ASSETS less the CURRENT LIABILITIES. Other measures include the liquidity RATIOS: the CURRENT RATIO and the QUICK RATIO (acid test). However, all these measures are most useful when seen in the context of similar companies and when looking at a trend for a particular company.

But when times are bad and the breath of fear has already chilled the markets, the banker must be cautious, conservative, and severe. His business has been aptly compared to that of a man who stands ready to lend umbrellas when it is fine and demand them back when it starts to rain.

Sir Geoffrey Crowther (1907–72), *An Outline of Money*, 1940, ch. 2

LISTED COMPANY

A COMPANY whose SHARES are listed or quoted on a

STOCK EXCHANGE. This means that there is an organised and substantial market in its shares, such that they can always be bought or sold. Stock exchanges have listing requirements concerning behaviour and the financial disclosures that listed companies must make.

In order to be listed a company must be a PUBLIC COMPANY in the UK, or registered with the SECURITIES AND EXCHANGE COMMISSION in the United States. In most countries there are many public companies that are not listed. Such unlisted companies may have decided to be public so that their shares may be bought and sold in less major markets than stock exchanges.

LOAN CAPITAL

There are many expressions for long-term loans: debt CAPITAL, loan STOCK, DEBENTURES, fixed INTEREST capital. Loans may be made by private persons, other businesses or banks. In many cases there is a market in loan securities, so that they can be sold to other investors by the original lender. The loans will usually have a fixed repayment, redemption or maturity date, and a fixed interest entitlement until that date.

Loans will normally be recorded in the borrowing COMPANY'S BALANCE SHEET, at the value of the issue proceeds, as long-term LIABILITIES. However, their value in the securities market at any moment will depend upon their interest rate and maturity date, and upon the market rate of interest at that moment.

> *Creditor*, n. *One of a tribe of savages dwelling beyond the Financial Straits and dreaded for their desolating incursions.*
> Ambrose Bierce (1842–1914?), *The Devil's Dictionary*, 1911

LOWER OF COST AND MARKET

A well-established rule for the valuation of CURRENT ASSETS, particularly STOCKS (INVENTORIES). In conventional accounting, COST means the historical purchase price of the stock, plus the costs of work done on it. In the UK, market value means NET REALISABLE VALUE (NRV), which is what the stock could be sold for in the normal course of business when ready for sale (less any expected costs involved in finishing and selling it).

The reason for this rule is CONSERVATISM. This suggests that, since the business intends to sell the stock fairly soon, its value should not be held above its expected selling price. However, it should also not be held above its cost since this would be to anticipate profits. Normally, in a successful business and particularly if prices are rising, cost will be used, because it will be below NRV. However, certain items of slow-moving or damaged stock will be reduced to NRV.

For FIXED ASSETS, which the business does not intend to sell, the NRV is normally ignored as irrelevant, in favour of the historical cost.

MAINSTREAM CORPORATION TAX

An element of the UK tax system since 1973. Mainstream corporation tax (MCT) is the amount of the CORPORATION TAX liability (CTL) for a year that has not already been paid as the ADVANCE CORPORATION TAX (ACT) connected to a dividend payment. Thus MCT = CTL − ACT. The MCT is paid nine months after a company's year end. MCT is not allowed to fall below zero. In 1997 proposals to abolish ACT were announced.

MANAGEMENT ACCOUNTING

A system designed specifically to serve the needs of the managers of a business, distinct from other work done by accountants, such as AUDITING or financial accounting. Financial accounting and reporting is required by law (and is intended for shareholders and CREDITORS) or by the need to deal with other parties such as customers or suppliers. Thus it has to obey many rules and has to strive for OBJECTIVITY. Management accounting, however, can be tailor-made for a particular COMPANY and will be designed to help managers to make decisions. It may involve many estimates and forecasts.

Nowadays it isn't sufficient to be a good innkeeper; you must become a cost accountant too.
Arthur Hailey, *Hotel*, 1965, ch. 10

MANAGEMENT BUY-OUT

The purchase of a COMPANY, as a GOING CONCERN, by members of its management.

MANAGEMENT LETTER

A letter from the auditors of a COMPANY to its directors or senior managers concerning audit findings, including the adequacy of control systems, the application of accounting principles, organisational efficiency, and so on.

MARGINAL COST

The extra cost that would result from producing

one extra unit of a product (strictly speaking an infinitesimally small amount extra). For the purpose of calculating marginal cost, all the FIXED COSTS should be ignored; only those extra costs that are related to the small production increase should be measured. For decision-making purposes it is often useful to compare the marginal cost of extra production with the marginal revenue that would result.

If cost accounting sets out, determined to discover what the cost of everything is and convinced in advance that there is one figure which can be found and which will furnish exactly the information which is desired for every possible purpose, it will necessarily fail, because there is no such figure. If it finds a figure which is right for some purposes it must necessarily be wrong for others.

J. Maurice Clark (1884–1963), *Studies in the Economics of Overhead Costs*, 1923, p. 14

MARKET CAPITALISATION
The total value of the SHARES of a COMPANY at a particular moment, as found by multiplying the number of its shares by the market price. In some newspapers, market capitalisation is published next to share prices.

MATCHING
A convention that the EXPENSES and REVENUES measured in order to calculate the PROFIT for a period should be those that relate to the period, rather than those for which cash has been paid or received. This is sometimes called the ACCRUALS CONCEPT. For example, accountants record a sale on CREDIT when it would be legally enforceable or on delivery of goods, not at the later date when cash is received. Similarly, the electricity expense of a business will be the amount that relates to the period, not what happened to be paid in the period.

DEPRECIATION is a good example of the matching concept in action. When a fixed asset is bought it will normally be used for several years. Thus accountants do not charge an expense equal to the cost of the asset in the year of purchase. Instead the asset is capitalised, recorded in the BALANCE SHEET and gradually charged as an expense, called depreciation, over the years of its use.

MATERIALITY

A strong concept which means that rules need not be strictly applied to unimportant amounts. For example, some companies may have small amounts of particular REVENUES, EXPENSES, ASSETS or LIABILITIES which would normally be separately disclosed in the financial statements. This need not be done if they are immaterial in size. The omission of such trivial amounts will help to make the statements clearer. Materiality is also to be seen at work in the extensive rounding of numbers in financial statements. Similarly, approximate measurement or valuation methods may be used if the end result is close to that which would be arrived at by stricter practices.

There is no precise definition of what is material. However, an item is immaterial if omission or mistreatment of it would not alter a reader's assessment of the financial statements. As a rule of thumb, this might be expressed as a few per cent of TURNOVER or PROFIT.

MCT

See MAINSTREAM CORPORATION TAX.

MEMORANDUM OF ASSOCIATION

A legal document drawn up as part of the registration of a COMPANY in the UK. The memorandum includes a record of the company's name, its registered office, its purpose and its AUTHORISED SHARE CAPITAL.

The other document drawn up at the birth of a company is the ARTICLES OF ASSOCIATION. These are rules concerning the relationships of the company to the shareholders, the shareholders to each other, and so on.

MERGER ACCOUNTING

A method of accounting for a BUSINESS COMBINATION. In the United States it is in fairly frequent use under the name of POOLING OF INTERESTS. In the UK merger accounting is rarely used and only became legal in 1981, so it has been normal to use the ACQUISITION method for business combinations and the subsequent preparation of CONSOLIDATED FINANCIAL STATEMENTS. In the UK, according to FRS 6, merger accounting can only be used when no acquirer can be identified. No FAIR VALUE exercise is carried out when accounting for a business combination by merger accounting, and no GOODWILL is recognised.

Takeovers are for the public good, but that's not why I do it. I do it to make money.
Sir James Goldsmith, *Sunday Times*, September 8th 1985

MINORITY INTERESTS

This is an amount which arises in CONSOLIDATED FINANCIAL STATEMENTS when a SUBSIDIARY is not wholly owned. It represents the CAPITAL provided by, and earned for, group shareholders who are not parent company shareholders. Even if a subsidiary is partly owned by minority shareholders, accountants bring in 100% of all its ASSETS, LIABILITIES, EXPENSES and REVENUES when preparing consolidated financial statements. In such statements, the proportions of these attributable to the minority shareholders are separately recognised as minority interests.

MONETARY ASSETS

Those ASSETS that are denominated in money terms or have a face value. Cash or DEBTORS (accounts receivable) are examples of monetary assets. Non-monetary assets include land, buildings and equipment. The distinction between monetary and non-monetary assets is important for some systems of FOREIGN CURRENCY TRANSLATION and INFLATION ACCOUNTING.

MONETARY WORKING CAPITAL ADJUSTMENT

One of the adjustments made to HISTORICAL COST
ACCOUNTING profit in certain systems of CURRENT
COST ACCOUNTING in order to take account of
changing prices. Monetary working capital adjustment is designed to adjust for the extra money
tied up in TRADE DEBTORS (net of TRADE CREDITORS)
as a result of the rise in price of STOCKS.

MONEY MEASUREMENT CONVENTION

Traditionally, accountants only include items in
ACCOUNTS and financial statements that can be
measured in money terms with reasonable OBJECT-
IVITY. Thus the value of a skilled management
team, or of loyal staff or customers, is not normally shown in financial statements. This is
because it is difficult to measure reliably its worth
in money terms. This convention is linked to the
use of HISTORICAL COST ACCOUNTING, where ASSETS
are measured at their purchase price or production cost.

MUTUAL FUNDS

The US name for financial institutions that use
money provided by investors to own and manage
a portfolio of investment in other STOCKS and
SHARES. The UK equivalent is UNIT TRUSTS.

NBV

See NET BOOK VALUE.

NET ASSETS

The worth of a business in accounting terms, as measured from its BALANCE SHEET. That is, it is the total of all the ASSETS, less the LIABILITIES that are owed to outsiders. Naturally this total equals the shareholders' EQUITY.

However, in reality a business is nearly always worth more than its net assets, because accountants will have been using HISTORICAL COST ACCOUNTING as a measurement basis, and because important assets, such as the loyalty of customers, will have been excluded because of the CONSERVATISM and MONEY MEASUREMENT conventions. Thus the MARKET CAPITALISATION of a COMPANY will nearly always be greater than its accounting net assets.

NET BOOK VALUE

The amount at which an asset is stated in the BALANCE SHEET of a business. This will depend upon the system of accounting being used, and is unlikely to be directly related to what the asset could be sold for. Conventional accounting measures assets at their net historical cost of purchase or production. The reason for the word "net" is that most FIXED ASSETS are gradually written off over their useful lives by amounts of DEPRECIATION. Thus the net book value (NBV) is usually the historical cost less accumulated charges of depreciation.

NET CURRENT ASSETS

The net current assets or working capital of a business is the excess of the CURRENT ASSETS (such as cash, STOCKS and DEBTORS) over the CURRENT LIABILITIES (such as TRADE CREDITORS and overdrafts). This is one measure of the LIQUIDITY of the business. However, the movement of the total from year to year, or of the CURRENT RATIO (of CURRENT ASSETS to CURRENT LIABILITIES) might be more useful information.

NET INCOME
The US expression for NET PROFIT.

NET PRESENT VALUE
Normally used in the context of the net present value (NPV) method of investment appraisal, which compares projects (or judges the likely success of one project) by estimating all the future cash flows (in and out) that would result from them, including the initial investment as an outflow and any investment incentives as inflows. These flows are "discounted" to take account of the fact that money now is worth more than money later. Thus the method involves estimation of a discount rate and of many years' worth of future cash inflows and outflows.

NET PROFIT
The excess of all the REVENUES over all the EXPENSES of a business for a period. The PROFIT AND LOSS ACCOUNT of a business will show the net PROFIT both before and after tax and the net profit after EXTRAORDINARY ITEMS. This profit is then available for distribution as DIVIDENDS (assuming that there is sufficient cash and that no past losses have to be covered first) or for transfer to various RESERVES. After any MINORITY INTERESTS and dividends on PREFERENCE SHARES have been deducted, the figure may be called EARNINGS.

NET REALISABLE VALUE
The amount that could be raised by selling an asset, less the costs of the sale. Net realisable value (NRV) usually implies a sale in the normal course of trade. Thus there would also be a deduction for any costs to bring the asset into a saleable state.

The normal rule for the valuation of CURRENT ASSETS, such as STOCKS, is to use the LOWER OF COST AND MARKET, where the latter means the NRV (except that, in the United States, it can mean the replacement cost, where lower).

The use of NRV has also been proposed for some systems of INFLATION ACCOUNTING, either as the main valuation basis or as a basis for those ASSETS that are about to be sold.

NET WORTH

See NET ASSETS.

NOMINAL LEDGER

An expression that is often used now to mean the main BOOKS of account in which the DOUBLE ENTRY records of the business are stored. Originally, the only records kept would have related to amounts owed to or by people. These would have been recorded on pieces of paper in a personal ledger. Later there would have been records of land and property in the real ledger; and of things that were ACCOUNTS in name only, such as INTEREST or electricity EXPENSES, in the nominal ledger. However, the term nominal ledger has now supplanted the others in the UK, and it remains in use even where all the information is actually on a computer disk or tape rather than in the traditional big black book.

NOMINAL VALUE

All SHARES in the UK have a nominal or PAR VALUE. This is usually little more than a label to distinguish a share from other types of shares issued by the same COMPANY. However, it does denote the extent of a shareholder's liability in the event of liquidation. Normally, the shares will be exchanged at above the nominal value, and the company will consequently issue any new shares at approximately the market price, leading to the recording of a SHARE PREMIUM account.

DIVIDENDS are expressed as a percentage of nominal value; and share capital is recorded at nominal value, any excess being recorded as share premium (PAID-IN SURPLUS in the United States).

NON-EQUITY SHARES

A UK expression for SHARES that are redeemable or have restrictions on their rights to DIVIDENDS or to participation in a surplus on the WINDING-UP of a COMPANY.

NON-PROFIT

The description applied to an organisation whose main aims are not commercial; for example, a university or a charity. Depending on the legal structure of such bodies, they may not be subject to normal accounting rules, though they may well be subject to other special rules. Such an organisation will usually prepare a BALANCE SHEET, but will not prepare a PROFIT AND LOSS ACCOUNT. It may instead prepare an INCOME AND EXPENDITURE ACCOUNT which still uses the MATCHING convention and other normal accounting rules, but arrives at a surplus or deficit rather than a PROFIT or loss. Alternatively, it may abandon the matching convention in favour of cash accounting, when it will prepare a RECEIPTS AND PAYMENTS ACCOUNT.

NPV

See NET PRESENT VALUE.

NRV

See NET REALISABLE VALUE.

O

OBJECTIVITY

An accounting measurement is said to be object-ive if it is reasonably independent of the judgment of accountants. There is much to be said for objec-tivity in accounting, because it reduces the time taken both to arrive at figures and to check them. It also means that the readers of financial state-ments can be more easily reassured that the fig-ures contained in them are not arbitrary.

The most obvious result of this desire for a sim-ple, checkable system is the conventional use of HISTORICAL COST ACCOUNTING. The original purchase price of an asset is much more objective than its current selling price, replacement cost or the value of future benefits expected to flow from it. However, such techniques as DEPRECIATION and PROVISIONS for BAD DEBTS do add subjectivity, even to historical cost accounting.

The main problem with greater objectivity is the possible sacrifice of relevance. The price of a machine eight years ago is objective, but irrel-evant for a knowledge about how much the machine is worth or for a decision about what to do with it.

A well-known saying in accounting is that it may be better to be approximately right than pre-cisely wrong. Nevertheless, at present, most of the world settles for a system that might be said to be not even precisely wrong.

Accounting: a respectable, conscious or unconscious way of disclosing, hiding or misrepresenting financial information to give a skilfully adapted economic picture of a company or its components.

Paulsson Frenckner, address to the 7th Annual Congress of the European Accounting Association, Saint-Gall, Switzerland, 1984

OFF-BALANCE SHEET FINANCE

One example of off-balance sheet finance is the existence of finance leases that are not treated as ASSETS and LIABILITIES (capitalised). In the UK and the United States it is now necessary for capital or

---

finance leases to be capitalised as though owned, and for an equal liability to be created. This adjusts for the otherwise misleading off-balance sheet finance. It expresses SUBSTANCE OVER FORM and is an attempt to achieve FAIR PRESENTATION.

A further example of off-balance sheet finance would be the non-consolidation of controlled companies that are technically not subsidiaries.

OPERATING AND FINANCIAL REVIEW

A statement which UK directors are encouraged to produce as part of a COMPANY'S ANNUAL REPORT. The review examines and explains important features of the company's financial position and results. The US equivalent is "management's discussion and analysis".

OPERATING LEASE

A LEASE which is treated by accountants as a rental rather than as a FINANCE LEASE.

OPERATING PROFIT

Operating profit means different things in different contexts. In conventional HISTORICAL COST ACCOUNTING it usually means the PROFIT before the deduction of INTEREST and tax, and possibly excluding gains from the letting of property or the sale of used machines. However, in the context of INFLATION ACCOUNTING, operating profit may mean something more complicated; that is, the historical cost profit, before interest and tax, adjusted for the effects of price changes on DEPRECIATION, COST OF SALES and, possibly, monetary working capital.

ORDINARY SHARES

The UK expression for the main type of ownership CAPITAL of companies. The US equivalent is COMMON STOCK. In a BALANCE SHEET the amount of money contributed by shareholders is split into issued share capital (at NOMINAL VALUE) and SHARE PREMIUM (for the excess amounts). A company will also have an AUTHORISED SHARE CAPITAL, as specified in its MEMORANDUM OF ASSOCIATION. This is a maximum potential share capital, which is disclosed as a note to the BALANCE SHEET.

An alternative type of share capital is PREFERENCE SHARES, but these have been unpopular in the UK since 1965 because of a change in the tax system.

OVERHEADS
EXPENSES of a business that cannot be traced to units of production or to processes that produce particular single products. The term "INDIRECT COSTS" has the same meaning. Obvious examples of overheads include the computer used by the head office, the salaries of factory managers, and the property taxes on the company's buildings. There will be production overheads, administration overheads, distribution overheads and possibly others.

OVER-THE-COUNTER SECURITIES
A method of allowing the exchange of securities for those companies that are not large enough for a full listing on a STOCK EXCHANGE, or for companies that would prefer not to obey the listing requirements of an exchange.

OWN SHARES
Until the 1981 Companies Act it was not possible for a UK company to purchase back its own ORDINARY SHARES from its shareholders. That rule was designed to protect CREDITORS. However, many countries did allow this; in the United States own shares may be held by a company and are called TREASURY STOCK. The UK joined the others, partly in order to allow private companies to buy out troublesome minorities of their shareholders who could not find buyers. When own shares are bought back, a transfer of distributable PROFIT must be made to an undistributable CAPITAL REDEMPTION RESERVE. This fulfils the function of protecting the creditors.

Pacioli, Luca

Fra Luca Pacioli is the most famous man in the history of accounting. He lived between about 1445 and about 1513. He was professor of mathematics at various Italian universities, and was a Franciscan friar (hence his title "Fra" for *frater*, that is brother). He was a friend of popes, princes and artists, including Leonardo da Vinci who drew the famous Proportions of Man as an illustration for one of Pacioli's books.

His is the earliest surviving major treatise on DOUBLE ENTRY. It is to be found in a book published in Venice in 1494, *Summa de Arithmetica, Geometria, Proportioni et Proportionalità*. This work had immense influence on the spread of double entry, as it was gradually adapted and translated into several languages. Pacioli was certainly not the inventor of double entry (by about 200 years) but his book did much to popularise it.

As the proverb says: "Frequent accounting makes for lasting friendship".
Luca Pacioli (*c*.1445–*c*.1517), *Particularis de Computis et Scripturis*, 1494, ch. 29

Paid-in surplus

A US expression for part of the amounts of money paid by investors when they purchase a COMPANY'S SHARES. Most shares in the United States have a PAR VALUE, which is a sort of label. Usually shares are issued at above par value, in which case the CAPITAL paid in is divided into share capital (at par) and paid-in surplus (the excess above par). For most purposes paid-in surplus is treated exactly as if it were share capital. There are several alternative titles for these amounts, including paid-in capital. In the UK the equivalent term is SHARE PREMIUM.

Par value

The normal US expression for the label attached to a share, that helps to distinguish it from other types of SHARES of the same COMPANY. The term is also used in the UK, where NOMINAL VALUE is an equivalent expression. Share capital is recorded at par, although the issue price, after the company is formed, is usually in excess of par because the market price for existing shares is generally higher. The excess amounts over par are called SHARE PREMIUM.

PARENT COMPANY

Generally a COMPANY that controls another company (its SUBSIDIARY). The normal financial reporting treatment is to prepare CONSOLIDATED FINANCIAL STATEMENTS for the group containing the parent and the subsidiaries.

PARTNERSHIP

A business arrangement whereby several people pool their capital and skills, and share the risks and profits. Normally, most or all of the partners are directly involved in the management of the business, unlike many companies where most shareholders are not part of management. In the UK and the United States partners are fully liable (they do not have limited liability) for the debts of the business, which is partly why they all wish to be involved in the management. Also, in the US and the UK except for Scotland, partnerships are not legal entities, so the partners not the partnership are taken to court in any legal action. In continental Europe there are several different forms of partnerships and many do have a legal personality.

PAY-BACK METHOD

A popular technique for appraising the likely success of projects, or for choosing between projects. It involves the analysis of their expected future net cash inflows, followed by a calculation of how many years it will take for the original CAPITAL investment to be recovered. It is popular because it is simple to use and, perhaps more importantly, simple to explain to non-financial managers.

It may be a reasonable way of choosing between projects which have similar expected patterns of CASH FLOW and similar initial investments. However, there are drawbacks to the more general use of the method:

1 It ignores the net cash flows that arise after the pay-back period; the quicker pay-back project may actually be far less profitable in total.

2 It ignores the time value of money; that is, it ignores the fact that money received in two years' time is less valuable than an equal amount received in one year's time.

More sophisticated methods of investment appraisal, such as the NET PRESENT VALUE method, adjust for both the above problems by discounting all the expected future income flows. However, these methods are not popular with business people, presumably because they are more difficult to understand and involve many more judgments. The pay-back method is often used in conjunction with others.

PENSION FUND
ASSETS set aside for the eventual payment of the PENSION OBLIGATION.

PENSION LIABILITIES/PROVISION
The amount shown in a BALANCE SHEET representing future payments to pensioners. The amount will be calculated after netting the PENSION FUND against the PENSION OBLIGATION (which is generally discounted).

PENSION OBLIGATION
The future expected payments to pensioners as a result of rights built up by services already rendered.

P/E RATIO
See PRICE/EARNINGS RATIO.

PLAN COMPTABLE
An accounting plan, that is the fundamental set of instructions for accounting practices in France,

Belgium, Spain and some developing countries. In France the *plan comptable général* contains:

- a standard decimalised CHART OF ACCOUNTS;
- the instructions relating to the presentation of uniform published financial statements;
- standard definitions of items and their valuation methods.

POOLING OF INTERESTS

See MERGER ACCOUNTING.

POST BALANCE SHEET EVENTS

A BALANCE SHEET is drawn up at a particular point in time, perhaps December 31 each year. Thus the events that occur after that date might be thought to be irrelevant in its presentation. However, events of material size may be included in one of two ways, assuming that they happen before the balance sheet is finalised by the COMPANY and its auditors:

1 Something may happen that makes clear a situation that already existed at the balance sheet date. For example, a doubtful debt may prove good after all. In this case the unnecessary provision for doubtful debts can be written back to PROFIT.

2 There may be an event that would affect the interpretation given to the financial statements. For example, several of the company's buildings may burn down after the balance sheet date. Such an event would not cause an adjustment to the financial statements, but would be recorded in the notes to them.

PRE-ACQUISITION PROFITS

Profits of a SUBSIDIARY company that had been earned before the COMPANY was purchased by its present parent company. Thus undistributed pre-acquisition profits are not seen as reserves of that group in CONSOLIDATED FINANCIAL STATEMENTS. Group RESERVES are calculated as the undistributed profits of the parent company, plus the group's share of undistributed post-acquisition profits of the consolidated companies.

PREFERENCE SHARES

SHARES normally having preference over ORDINARY SHARES for dividend payments and for the return of CAPITAL if a COMPANY is wound up. That is, ordinary DIVIDENDS cannot be paid in a particular year until the preference dividend, which is usually a fixed percentage, has been paid. Further, it is usual for preference shares (known as preferred stock in the United States) to be cumulative, that is for any unpaid dividends to cumulate into future years and to remain preferential to any ordinary dividend. The disadvantage for preference shareholders is that, if a company is successful, the ordinary dividend will be expected to rise over the years, whereas the preference dividend will not.

Tax changes in the UK in 1965 made preference shares much less attractive than fixed INTEREST loans, because the interest on the latter is tax deductible for companies whereas dividends are not. Thus preference share capital has become quite rare.

PREFERRED STOCK

See PREFERENCE SHARES.

PRELIMINARY EXPENSES

The EXPENSES relating to the setting up of a COMPANY, such as those relating to the issue of SHARES or the preparation of legal documents, are not allowed to be capitalised (shown as ASSETS) in either the UK or the United States. They must thus be treated as expenses immediately. In some other countries, such as several continental European countries, these expenses can be capitalised as assets and gradually depreciated.

PREPAYMENTS

Amounts recorded in a BALANCE SHEET which show that certain payments have been made in advance, perhaps for rent, property taxes or insurance premiums. Conventional accounting uses the

ACCRUALS CONCEPT or MATCHING principle, which is that only the EXPENSES that relate to a period should be charged against PROFIT for that period. Thus prepayments will have been paid in the period leading up to the balance sheet, but will not be treated as expenses until a subsequent period. Technically, instead of the DEBIT being treated as an expense, it is treated as an asset.

The parallel treatment for expenses paid late gives rise to accrued expenses on the balance sheet.

PRESENT VALUE

The future net cash inflows expected from an asset or a proposed project, discounted to reflect the fact that money is more valuable if received now rather than later. For the valuation of an asset it might be more normal to refer to the method as the ECONOMIC VALUE. This makes an appearance as a possible valuation in unusual circumstances under some systems of INFLATION ACCOUNTING. When choosing between investment projects, these concepts are normally considered under the heading of NET PRESENT VALUE.

PRICE/EARNINGS RATIO

The price/earnings or P/E ratio has become exceptionally important in the late 20th century as a rapid means of summing up the way in which investors view a particular COMPANY. The ratio at any moment compares the market price of an ordinary share in the company with the EARNINGS PER SHARE of that company, based on the most recently available year's figure for the PROFIT after INTEREST, tax, MINORITY INTEREST and preference dividend.

A high P/E ratio means that a share is expected to perform well in the future. Investors must deem it to be worth paying a large multiple of the earnings for the share because of their high expectations. However, this is no help in deciding which share to buy; it merely shows which shares are well thought of. They are of course more expensive. For large stock exchanges, such as those of

London and New York, there is considerable evidence that available information is rapidly taken into account in share prices (this is called the EFFICIENT MARKET HYPOTHESIS). Thus there should be no share that is obviously good value; good shares will command good prices.

PRIOR-YEAR ADJUSTMENT

This may come about if a business discovers an error of material size in its financial statements of previous years, or if there is a change in accounting policies because of new laws, standards or circumstances. It is UK practice under FRS 3 to adjust the BALANCE SHEET of the previous year to take account of such events. This is because any changes that result are deemed not to be economic events of the current year, and thus not to be suitable items for a PROFIT AND LOSS ACCOUNT.

PRIVATE COMPANY

As registered under UK COMPANY LAW, a private COMPANY is one that is not allowed to sell its SHARES or loan STOCK on an open market. Such a company has "limited" or an abbreviation as part of its name, as opposed to "public limited company" for a PUBLIC COMPANY. The vast majority of UK companies are private companies; there are about 950,000 of them.

The company law relating to private companies is slightly less onerous than that for public companies. For example, private companies under certain size limits are exempted from some annual publication requirements; and private companies have a slightly less restrictive definition of distributable PROFIT.

PROFIT

In accounting terms, the excess of the REVENUES over the EXPENSES of the period. The revenues and expenses are those that relate to the period, rather than necessarily those that were received or paid in cash in the period. That is, the MATCHING convention is followed.

PROFIT AND LOSS ACCOUNT

The financial statement that summarises the difference between the REVENUES and EXPENSES of a period. Such statements may be drawn up frequently for the managers of a business, but a full audited statement is normally only published for each accounting year. The equivalent US expression is INCOME STATEMENT.

Publication of profit and loss accounts was first made compulsory for companies in the UK by the 1929 Companies Act. There is now a choice of formats among the four set out in the 1985 Companies Act. It is normal for UK companies to choose a vertical or statement format, rather than a two-sided or account format. For private companies below a certain size there are some exemptions from publication requirements.

> *Profits are not due to risks, but to superior skill in taking risks. They are not subtracted from the gains of labour but are earned, in the same sense in which the wages of skilled labour are earned.*
> Frank A. Fetter (1863–1949),
> *The Principles of Economics*, 1904, p. 291

PROFITABILITY

This is not the same as the PROFIT of a business. A profit of a particular size may be impressive for a corner grocery shop, but unimpressive for a large multinational company. Measures of profitability try to put the profit into the context of the size of the business. Thus profitability is normally a measure of the return on CAPITAL invested in the business. One possible ratio of profitability is of NET PROFIT before INTEREST and tax to the total long-term finance of the business. Another ratio is the net profit after interest and tax to the shareholders' EQUITY.

Such RATIOS become useful when one COMPANY can be compared with another or with the average for its industry; or when one company's ratio can be seen in the context of the ratios for previous years. In all cases it is important to try to compare ratios that have been defined consistently.

PROPORTIONAL CONSOLIDATION

A technique used in some countries as part of the preparation of CONSOLIDATED FINANCIAL STATEMENTS for a group of companies. It brings into the consolidated financial statements the group's share of all the ASSETS, LIABILITIES, REVENUES and EXPENSES of the partly owned COMPANY. The method is used by companies in France (and to some extent in several other countries) for dealing with investments in companies that are held on a JOINT VENTURE basis with one or more other investing companies. In the UK and the United States, joint venture companies are included in consolidated statements by the EQUITY METHOD.

PROSPECTUS

A document, used by potential investors, that precedes the issue of SHARES to the public. It outlines the financial position and prospects of the COMPANY, and gives details of the senior executives. Assistance with the preparation of the document will usually have been sought from merchant bankers or investment bankers, and independent accountants will report on its reasonableness. A summary of previous years' financial results will also be included.

PROVISIONS

Unfortunately, there is some vagueness about the use of the words provisions and reserves, despite definitions in COMPANY LAW. A provision in the UK usually means an amount charged against PROFIT to reduce the recorded value of an asset or to cover an expected liability, even if the exact amount or timing of the liability is uncertain. A reserve, however, is an amount voluntarily or compulsorily set aside out of profit (after the latter has been calculated), often to demonstrate that the amount is not to be distributed as DIVIDENDS (see RESERVES).

A company may have provisions for DEPRECIATION, for BAD DEBTS, for taxation or for law suits that are expected to go against the company. All these provisions, when they were set up or added to, would lead to a reduction in the reported profit figure. When the law suit is lost or the doubtful debt goes bad, the provision will be reduced, and (assuming that the provision was adequate) no further charge against profit will be needed.

Some potential losses are not at all likely, and it would be regarded as unduly conservative to make provisions for them. Instead they are recorded in the notes to the BALANCE SHEET as contingent LIABILITIES.

However, as mentioned above, usage of the words is loose. For example, it is not unknown for accountants and others to talk about a "bad debt reserve"; and in some continental European countries there may be large "provisions for CONTINGENCIES" that Anglo-Saxon practice would treat as reserves. In US terminology ALLOWANCES is often used instead of provisions, and an amount set aside to cover an expected liability could be called a reserve.

The accountant transcends the conservatism of the proverb, "Do not count your chickens before they are hatched", saying "Here are a lot of chickens already safely hatched, but for the love of Mike, use discretion and don't count them all for perhaps some will die."

H.R. Hatfield (1866–1945), *Accounting*, 1927, p. 256, n. 13

PRUDENCE

A concept that is strong in the accounting practices of nearly all countries. As the term suggests, it implies being cautious in the valuation of ASSETS or the measurement of PROFIT. It means always taking the lowest reasonable estimate of the value of assets; always anticipating losses but never anticipating profits.

In ACCOUNTING STANDARDS (SSAP 2) and company law, prudence may be found as a compulsory, fundamental principle. However, the word "conservatism" is also in use, sometimes meaning a slightly stricter version of prudence. An example of prudence is the use of the LOWER OF COST AND MARKET rule for the valuation of STOCKS (INVENTORIES).

PUBLIC COMPANY

A COMPANY whose securities (SHARES and loan STOCK) may be publicly traded. In the UK the legal form of such a company is set out in the Companies Act. The company must have "public limited company" (or plc) as part of its name. There are equivalents to this form in other European countries (see COMPANY – Table 7). In the United States the nearest equivalent is a corporation that is registered with the SECURITIES AND EXCHANGE COMMISSION.

There are about 12,000 companies in the plc form, under 2,000 of which are listed on the London STOCK EXCHANGE. Public companies have to obey slightly stricter rules than private companies. For example, there are no exemptions from the publication requirements of the Companies Act, as apply to smaller private companies. There is also a slightly more restrictive definition of distributable PROFIT.

PURCHASE

A US term for the normal method of BUSINESS COMBINATION. In the UK this would be called an ACQUISITION.

QUALIFIED AUDIT REPORT

This does not refer to the qualifications of the auditors, although COMPANY LAW in the UK and the SECURITIES AND EXCHANGE COMMISSION in the United States do indeed require companies to be audited by independent qualified accountants. A qualified audit report is one which states (in the UK) that the financial statements give a TRUE AND FAIR VIEW except that or subject to certain qualifying remarks. The qualifications may concern the infringement of company law or ACCOUNTING STANDARDS. If there are sufficiently serious problems the auditors may withhold their opinion (perhaps because of major uncertainties) or give an adverse opinion.

QUALIFYING DEGREE

An academic degree that allows entry to the training programmes or exemption from some examinations of professional accountancy bodies (see RELEVANT DEGREE).

QUARTERLY REPORTING

Companies registered with the SECURITIES AND EXCHANGE COMMISSION in the United States (the approximate equivalent of public companies in the UK) are required to do more than present extensive disclosures in their ANNUAL REPORT. They also have to make quarterly reports on TURNOVER, GROSS PROFIT and NET PROFIT. The closest UK parallel is the London STOCK EXCHANGE requirement for an unaudited, half-yearly INTERIM REPORT.

QUASI-SUBSIDIARY

The UK expression (in FRS 5) for an undertaking which should be treated as a SUBSIDIARY for the purposes of accounting because it is controlled for benefit by another COMPANY, even though it is not legally a subsidiary.

QUICK RATIO

A COMPANY's quick ratio (or acid test) is a measure of its LIQUIDITY. The ratio is normally measured by comparing the cash plus DEBTORS of a company with its CURRENT LIABILITIES. An alternative measure (of all CURRENT ASSETS to all current liabilities) is called the CURRENT RATIO.

QUOTED COMPANY

An alternative expression for a LISTED COMPANY, that is a COMPANY whose name appears on the list of a STOCK EXCHANGE. Such a company must be a PUBLIC COMPANY (plc) in the UK, or registered with the SECURITIES AND EXCHANGE COMMISSION in the United States.

Corporation, n. *An ingenious device for obtaining individual profit without individual responsibility.*

Ambrose Bierce (1842–1914?), *The Devil's Dictionary,* 1911

R&D
See RESEARCH AND DEVELOPMENT.

RATE OF RETURN
A measure of the PROFITABILITY of a business. It normally compares the annual PROFIT of the business with the amount of CAPITAL invested in it. The rate of return may be measured before tax or after tax, and it is important to be clear which one it is. Such a measure will normally be used to compare one COMPANY with another. Thus it is also important to define the profit figure and the capital or asset base carefully.

RATIOS
Ratio analysis is a popular sport of investment analysts, financial journalists, textbook writers and examination setters. It involves the comparison of a COMPANY with its past or with other companies, by setting one piece of financial data in the context of another. For example, comparison of the absolute levels of PROFIT for two companies of different sizes would obviously be meaningless. However, it may be valuable when the profits of the two companies can be set in the context of their total ASSETS or CAPITAL figures. This would lead to a comparison of PROFITABILITY ratios. There are also the GEARING RATIO, which measures the proportion of debt finance; the LIQUIDITY ratio, which measures the size of current assets in the context of the debts of a company; and the frequently used PRICE/EARNINGS RATIO, which sets the market price of an ordinary or common share in the context of its part of the annual EARNINGS of the company.

Like most useful simplifications, ratio analysis contains great dangers. First, it is important to ensure that there is consistency of definition from year to year and from company to company. When international comparisons are being made ratio analysis is especially dangerous, because there are major differences in the methods used for valuing assets and measuring profits.

Another danger is that ideal ratios may be

thought to exist. An example is the liquidity ratio. There are textbooks which suggest that a CURRENT RATIO (that is, CURRENT ASSETS:CURRENT LIABILITIES) should be above 2:1. However, it is nonsense to regard this as a general rule. For some companies in some industries (possibly heavy engineering), this level might be dangerously low; for other companies (such as supermarket chains) it would suggest exceptional inefficiency in the use of resources.

REAL GAIN

Normally the word "real" in the context of accounting or economics implies an amount that has been corrected for inflation. Thus a real gain is one that has been reduced to the extent that it is due merely to the change in value of money (see INFLATION ACCOUNTING).

REALISABLE PROFIT

A PROFIT is realisable, but unrealised, if productive activity or price rises mean that ASSETS could be sold for more than they were previously recorded at in a COMPANY'S ACCOUNTS. Conventional HISTORICAL COST ACCOUNTING ignores realisable profits until they become objective and easily measurable by being realised, basically by sale. This is partly owing to traditional CONSERVATISM, and partly to the much greater simplicity and auditability of objective, realised amounts.

However, the problem that results from this REALISATION CONVENTION is that the profits recorded for any year are an incomplete indication of what happened in that year. To take a simple example, suppose that an asset is bought as an investment and that it is sold after ten years. In the first nine years no gains will be recorded, but in the tenth year the full gain will be treated as PROFIT even if the asset had actually lost value during that year.

REALISATION CONVENTION

A well-established principle of conventional accounting, that gains or profits should only be recognised when they have been objectively realised by a sale being agreed. This is consistent with the all-pervasive concept of CONSERVATISM, which anticipates losses but never profits.

REALISED PROFITS

Profits that have been objectively verified by the evidence of a sale or some other event (see REALISATION CONVENTION). Conventional accounting rests heavily upon the PRUDENCE and OBJECTIVITY that this allows. COMPANY LAW in the UK requires that only realised profits may be recorded in the PROFIT AND LOSS ACCOUNT. However, "realised" is to be interpreted in the context of "principles generally accepted" for accounting purposes. Thus the rules of ACCOUNTING STANDARDS will normally determine what is deemed to be realised.

Also UK company law requires that dividend distributions must not exceed accumulated realised profits less accumulated realised losses. Thus profits and DIVIDENDS cannot result from a plot of land that has been growing in value over many years until the land is sold.

RECEIPTS AND PAYMENTS ACCOUNT

For certain unincorporated enterprises, particularly those of a not-for-profit nature, conventional accounting, based on the MATCHING convention, may appear unnecessarily complicated. For them, a summary of cash amounts coming in or going out in a period may be sufficient. This summary is called a receipts and payments account.

As an example of the difference between this and conventional accounting, consider the purchase of a new photocopying machine that is expected to last for ten years. Accountants would normally charge an amount of DEPRECIATION each year for the using up of the machine. However, a receipts and payments account would merely show the amount paid for the machine in the year that it was paid.

NON-PROFIT organisations that are obliged or wish to retain the matching convention still produce an INCOME AND EXPENDITURE ACCOUNT in the UK or, in the United States, an INCOME STATEMENT.

These arrive at surpluses or deficits, rather than profits or losses.

RECEIVABLES
The US expression for amounts of money due to a business, often known as ACCOUNTS RECEIVABLE. The UK term is DEBTORS.

RECOVERABLE AMOUNT
The higher of the FAIR VALUE of an asset and the discounted expected future net cash receipts from it. The recoverable amount is used in some measures of IMPAIRMENT.

REDEEMABLE SHARES
SHARES that are allowed to be bought back by the COMPANY that originally issued them. In the UK most shares are not redeemable, whereas most loan STOCK or DEBENTURES are. However, there is legal provision for shares to be made redeemable, and this is normally used for preference shares. The irredeemable nature of most UK shares is designed to protect CREDITORS by ensuring that a company cannot pay CAPITAL back to shareholders unless it is wound up, when all other claims would take priority. Thus when UK shares are allowed to be redeemed, the conditions are strict, and amounts have to be transferred from distributable profits to UNDISTRIBUTABLE RESERVES (called capital redemption reserves).

REDUCING BALANCE DEPRECIATION
A technique for calculating the DEPRECIATION charge, usually for machines, whereby the annual charge reduces over the years of an asset's life. A fixed percentage depreciation is charged each year on the COST (first year) or the undepreciated cost (subsequent years).

REGISTRAR OF COMPANIES
A UK government official who is charged with the collection, organisation and granting of public access to the financial statements of companies.

REGULATION S-X

An important source of rules relating to the preparation of financial statements for those companies registered with the SECURITIES AND EXCHANGE COMMISSION in the United States.

RELATED PARTIES

Enterprises or people who have a relationship with the reporting entity. The exact definition will vary from country to country, but in the UK and the United States it includes subsidiaries, associated companies and relatives of the directors.

RELEVANT DEGREE

An academic degree that allows entry into the training programmes or exemption from some parts of the examinations of various accountancy bodies. In some cases the term QUALIFYING DEGREE is used instead. Normally such degrees contain financial accounting, MANAGEMENT ACCOUNTING, business finance, taxation, economics, law and statistics. Thus some degrees that might be thought to be relevant for the work of an accountant, such as a degree specialising in economics, will not be counted for this purpose.

REPLACEMENT COST ACCOUNTING

A system of preparing financial statements in which all ASSETS (and EXPENSES relating to them, such as DEPRECIATION) are valued at their CURRENT REPLACEMENT COST.

RESEARCH AND DEVELOPMENT

There has been controversy about how to account for research and development (R&D) EXPENSES. They are designed to bring benefit in future years, so it would seem unfair to charge all the expenses this year (when there are no related REVENUES), and to recognise the revenues in a later year (when there are no related expenses). Thus there is an argument for using the MATCHING principle, and for treating the expenditure as an asset (capitalising it), and only treating it as an expense in the future when the related revenue arrives. Unfortunately, this goes against the principle of PRUDENCE because it is impossible to be totally sure what (if any) the future revenue coming from present research and development will be.

In the UK the present standard (SSAP 13) allows some development expenditure (but not research) to be capitalised under certain prudent conditions. Development expenditure may be distinguished because it has a practical application to products or processes. In the United States and Germany such CAPITALISATION is not allowed. By contrast, in Japan and France both research and development can be capitalised.

RESERVES

An amount notionally set aside out of profits (after the latter have been calculated), often to register the fact that they are voluntarily or compulsorily undistributable. Reserves should be distinguished from PROVISIONS. In the UK the latter are charged in the calculation of PROFIT, and represent reductions in the value of ASSETS or anticipations of future LIABILITIES. Of course neither reserves nor provisions are amounts of cash. A provision involves an accounting expense, and a reserve is an accounting allocation of undistributed profit from one heading to another. Reserves belong to shareholders, and are part of a total of shareholders' EQUITY, which also includes share capital. This total is represented by all the assets of the business, less the liabilities owed to outsiders.

It should be noted that this terminology is used somewhat loosely by some accountants. In the United States "reserve" is used to cover some of the meanings of "provision" in the UK.

RESTRICTED SURPLUS

A US expression for amounts of past PROFIT that are unavailable for distribution to shareholders. The UK equivalent would be UNDISTRIBUTABLE RESERVES.

RETAINED EARNINGS

See RETAINED PROFIT.

RETAINED PROFIT

Amounts of PROFIT, earned in the year and former years, that have not yet been paid out as DIVIDENDS.

REVALUATION

Conventional accounting uses HISTORICAL COST ACCOUNTING as the basis for the valuation of ASSETS. However, in some countries, including the UK but not the United States, it is acceptable to revalue FIXED ASSETS, either annually or from time to time. These revaluations can be done on the basis of CURRENT REPLACEMENT COST or of NET REALISABLE VALUE. It is quite normal for large UK companies to show land and buildings at revalued amounts in their balance sheets. Clearly, the purpose of this is to avoid a seriously misleading impression of their worth when prices have risen substantially.

REVENUES

The revenues of an accounting period are those receipts of any period that relate to the accounting period. An analogous definition applies to EXPENSES and payments. This is called the ACCRUALS CONVENTION or MATCHING. For example, if an insurance COMPANY receives cash in 1997 for a 1998 insurance premium, the revenue will be recognised in 1998, not in the year of receipt. Similarly, when SALES are made to customers "on account" or "on CREDIT", these sales are recognised immediately, rather than waiting until the cash arrives.

REVENUE RESERVE

A rather old-fashioned UK expression for amounts of RETAINED PROFIT that are available for distribution as DIVIDENDS.

REVIEW PANEL

A committee which is part of the standard-setting and enforcement machinery introduced in the UK in 1990. The Financial Reporting Review Panel investigates suspected breaches of COMPANY LAW (including the failure of ACCOUNTS to give a TRUE AND FAIR VIEW), which are referred to it. The panel can then take companies to court under procedures introduced by the 1989 Companies Act.

RIGHTS ISSUE

The sale of additional SHARES by a COMPANY to its existing shareholders. The rights to buy the shares, at slightly lower than the market price in order to ensure a full sale, are given out in proportion to the existing holdings. Thus the existing group of shareholders may be largely preserved. Since the sale is to existing shareholders, the advertisement and PROSPECTUS preparations need not be so expensive as for issues to the public. So rights issues are cheaper and more popular than other means of selling new shares.

Rights issues should be distinguished from BONUS SHARES, CAPITALISATION or scrip issues, where no money is paid to the company, but where existing shareholders receive a proportionate amount of free extra shares and distributable profits are relabelled as share CAPITAL.

SALE-AND-LEASEBACK

A method of raising funds by a COMPANY without immediately depleting resources or incurring LIABILITIES. If a company owns and uses FIXED ASSETS, it may find it advantageous, for tax or other reasons, to sell them to a financial institution (the lessor) who then leases them back to the company.

SALES

The figure for sales, recorded in the financial statements for a period, will include all those sales agreed or delivered in the period, rather than those that are paid for in cash. The sales figure will be shown net of sales taxes (VAT in the UK). In the UK the word "TURNOVER" is used in the financial statements, although "sales" is generally used in the BOOKS of account.

SANDILANDS REPORT

The 1975 report by the UK government committee on INFLATION ACCOUNTING chaired by Sir Francis Sandilands. It recommended that a system of CURRENT COST ACCOUNTING be developed to take account of changing prices.

SCRIP ISSUE

See BONUS SHARES.

SEC

See SECURITIES AND EXCHANGE COMMISSION.

SECRET RESERVES

Various means by which a COMPANY, particularly a financial institution, can make its true financial strength unclear in its financial statements. The purpose of this is to build up resources in case of future difficulty. If that future difficulty eventually emerges, it may be possible to hide it completely by merely absorbing it with the secret RESERVES. This event may avoid a dangerous loss of confidence in the bank or other company concerned. Secret reserves may be created by deliberately allowing ASSETS to be undervalued, or by creating unnecessary PROVISIONS.

SECURITIES AND EXCHANGE COMMISSION

A US government agency set up in 1934 after the Wall Street Crash of 1929. Its function is to control the issue and exchange of publicly traded SHARES. Companies with such shares must register with the Securities and Exchange Commission (SEC) and then obey a mass of detailed regulations about disclosure and audit of financial information. An SEC-registered company in the United States is the nearest equivalent to a PUBLIC COMPANY (plc) in the UK. In neither country are all such companies listed on a STOCK EXCHANGE.

The SEC issues its own rules for financial reporting, such as REGULATION S-X, which requires annual financial statements and quarterly disclosure of SALES and PROFIT. Indeed, the only powerful requirements for disclosure and audit in the United States come from the SEC, directly or indirectly. The private body that sets accounting standards, the FINANCIAL ACCOUNTING STANDARDS BOARD, is given "substantial authoritative support" by the SEC. However, the latter sometimes intervenes directly in the setting of accounting rules.

The form that must be sent annually by registered companies to the SEC is called Form 10-K. This contains much accounting and economic information that supplements the published financial statements. The 10-K is available to the public. Foreign registrants who do not produce US GAAP statements must file FORM 20-F.

SEGMENTAL REPORTING

An analysis of SALES, PROFIT or ASSETS by line of business or by geographical area.

SFAS

See STATEMENTS OF FINANCIAL ACCOUNTING STANDARDS.

SHAREHOLDERS' FUNDS

The total of the shareholders' interest in a COMPANY. This will include the original share CAPITAL, amounts contributed in excess of the NOMINAL VALUE of SHARES (that is, SHARE PREMIUM), and RETAINED PROFITS and other RESERVES. In the United

States this total is sometimes called STOCKHOLDERS' EQUITY. The shareholders' funds will equal the NET ASSETS or net worth of the company.

SHARE PREMIUM

An amount paid into a COMPANY (by shareholders when they purchased SHARES from the company) in excess of the NOMINAL VALUE of the shares. Share premium may be treated for most purposes exactly as if it were share capital. Both are included in shareholders' EQUITY. One US equivalent is PAID-IN SURPLUS.

The shares are a penny, and ever so many are taken by
Rothschild and Baring.
And just as a few are allotted to you, you awake with a
shudder despairing.
W.S. Gilbert (1836–1911), *Iolanthe*, 1882, act II

SHARES

Parts of the ownership of a COMPANY. Shareholders jointly own a company. In the case of most companies, the shareholders have limited liability for the company's debts. Thus they are content to delegate the management of the company to boards of directors. Most of the share capital of a company will normally have been provided by the holders of ORDINARY SHARES (COMMON STOCK in the United States). These shareholders can exercise their votes at the company's ANNUAL GENERAL MEETING, when dividend decisions and much other business is done. They also share in the prosperity of the company because the DIVIDENDS and the share value may be expected to rise over the years.

Shares are recorded in financial statements at their NOMINAL VALUE or PAR VALUE, which distinguishes one type of share from another. Amounts paid in by shareholders who bought shares from the company at above par value are shown as SHARE PREMIUM (PAID-IN SURPLUS in the United States).

Shares are normally not redeemable by the company that issued them. However, most of the business of stock exchanges is done in the second-hand market for such securities. (See also PREFERENCE SHARES, BONUS SHARES and RIGHTS ISSUE.)

SIC
See STANDING INTERPRETATIONS COMMITTEE.

SOCIÉTÉ ANONYME
A French, Belgian, Luxembourg or Swiss PUBLIC COMPANY.

SOCIÉTÉ À RESPONSABILITÉ LIMITÉE
A French, Belgian, Luxembourg or Swiss PRIVATE COMPANY.

SOLVENCY
A business (or person) is solvent if it can pay its bills or accounts as they fall due. The likely ability of a business to do this can be measured by examining its LIQUIDITY.

SORP
See STATEMENTS OF RECOMMENDED PRACTICE.

SOURCE AND APPLICATION OF FUNDS
Statements of source and application of funds were once required as part of the financial statements of companies in the UK. They are also known as funds flow statements. The definition of "funds" was not clear, and these statements have now been superseded by the CASH FLOW STATEMENT.

SSAP
See STATEMENTS OF FINANCIAL ACCOUNTING STANDARDS.

STAG
A speculator on a STOCK EXCHANGE who buys newly issued securities in advance at a fixed price, presuming that there will be a shortage of them so that they can be rapidly sold when the price rises. (See also BEAR and BULL.)

STANDING INTERPRETATIONS COMMITTEE

The task of the Standing Interpretations Committee (SIC), set up in 1997 by the INTERNATIONAL ACCOUNTING STANDARDS COMMITTEE, is to publish interpretations of unclear details of existing international accounting standards.

STATEMENT OF PRINCIPLES

The UK version of a CONCEPTUAL FRAMEWORK.

STATEMENT OF TOTAL RECOGNISED GAINS AND LOSSES

A major financial statement required from UK companies since 1993. It includes gains and losses that are not recorded in the PROFIT AND LOSS ACCOUNT, such as those on FOREIGN CURRENCY TRANSLATION and on the REVALUATION OF FIXED ASSETS. (See also COMPREHENSIVE INCOME.)

STATEMENTS OF FINANCIAL ACCOUNTING CONCEPTS

Statements from the US FINANCIAL ACCOUNTING STANDARDS BOARD, issued as part of the search for a CONCEPTUAL FRAMEWORK. They deal with such matters as the objectives and elements of financial statements.

STATEMENTS OF FINANCIAL ACCOUNTING STANDARDS

The US term for ACCOUNTING STANDARDS as set by the FINANCIAL ACCOUNTING STANDARDS BOARD since its foundation in 1973. Statements of financial accounting standards (SFAS) are the technical rules of valuation, measurement and disclosure for financial statements.

STATEMENTS OF RECOMMENDED PRACTICE

UK documents with less authority than ACCOUNTING STANDARDS. Statements of recommended practice (SORP) are designed to deal with particular industries or with specialist technical problems, and are drafted by an industry or special interest group.

STATEMENTS OF STANDARD ACCOUNTING PRACTICE

The UK term for those ACCOUNTING STANDARDS

issued up to 1990, generally known by their acronym SSAP.

STEWARDSHIP

The original purpose of accounting; also called accountability. Kings or lords who were away at war or for other purposes would leave their estates in the hands of a steward. The steward would keep an account of the payments and receipts of the estate so that he could be discharged of responsibility when the owner returned. The steward would "render an account" to the owner, who might have been illiterate and had thus to hear it (audit derives from the Latin for "he hears").

Today shareholders are the owners of companies, and directors are their appointees, who look after the ASSETS in their absence. The annual financial statements need to be checked by independent experts (the auditors) and sent to the shareholders. Thus it may be seen whether the directors have been proper stewards.

In recent years the financial statements have come to be seen as the provision of information useful for taking decisions about whether to buy or sell a company's securities. This requires forward-looking information, whereas stewardship is essentially backward-looking. This conflict has led to difficulties in setting rules for, and in interpreting, financial statements. For example, it could be claimed that HISTORICAL COST ACCOUNTING was more useful for stewardship than for financial decision-making.

O my good lord
At many times I have brought in my accounts,
Laid them before you; you would throw them off,
And say you found them in mine honesty.
William Shakespeare (1564–1616), *Timon of Athens*,
1607–8, act II, sc. II

STOCK

The US term for securities of various kinds; for

example, COMMON STOCK or PREFERENCE STOCK (equivalent to ORDINARY SHARES and PREFERENCE SHARES in UK terminology). However, the word "share" is also understood in the United States, so that stockholder and shareholder are interchangeable. In the UK this meaning survives, particularly in the expressions STOCK EXCHANGE and loan stock.

A source of great confusion in Anglo-American conversation is the UK use of the word STOCKS for what are called INVENTORIES in the United States.

STOCK APPRECIATION RELIEF
A UK tax relief that operated between 1973 and 1984. It was designed to allow for the fact that reported profits included gains on the holding of STOCKS (INVENTORIES) that were merely a result of price increases.

STOCK DIVIDEND
The US terms stock dividend and stock split describe the issue of free extra SHARES to existing shareholders, combined with the CAPITALISATION of RETAINED EARNINGS. A stock dividend is an extra issue of up to about 25% of the number of existing shares and a stock split is an extra issue of over about 20%. The two issues are accounted for differently. The equivalent UK expressions are BONUS SHARES, capitalisation or scrip issues.

STOCK EXCHANGE
An organised market for the issue of new securities and the exchange of second-hand ones. Companies whose SHARES may be sold on such exchanges are called listed or quoted companies (see LISTED COMPANY). They must be public companies (in the UK) or registered with the SECURITIES AND EXCHANGE COMMISSION (in the United States). In addition to the normal accounting regulations, listed companies have to obey the listing requirements of their particular stock exchange. Such requirements may include extra disclosure of accounting data or of facts concerning their executives or their plans. In the UK it is the listing requirements of the London Stock Exchange that

call for half-yearly "interim" financial information.

STOCKHOLDERS' EQUITY

A US expression for the total stake in a COMPANY owned by the stockholders, including their invested CAPITAL and RETAINED EARNINGS. (See SHARE-HOLDERS' FUNDS, which is an expression more readily understood in the UK.)

STOCK SPLIT

See STOCK DIVIDEND.

STOCKS

As used in the UK, this word means the raw materials, work-in-progress and finished goods of a business. Unfortunately, in the United States the word INVENTORIES is used instead, and stocks means SHARES there.

The valuation of STOCKS (INVENTORIES) is an important exercise for a business. The figure usually forms an important part of the CURRENT ASSETS total on a BALANCE SHEET, and it is a vital part of the calculation of PROFIT. The GROSS PROFIT of a business is the SALES less the COST OF SALES. The cost of sales is the purchases of goods, adjusted for the change in the level of stocks during the period, plus certain costs.

The normal valuation method is to use the LOWER OF COST AND MARKET value. The use of COST is a normal method of accounting for all ASSETS under the HISTORICAL COST ACCOUNTING convention. However, because stocks are current assets and may soon be sold, their market value will also be relevant. The principle of PRUDENCE causes accountants to reduce the value of stocks below cost in those fairly unusual cases where market value has fallen below cost. "Market value" in the UK means NET REALISABLE VALUE.

Cost includes all the EXPENSES associated with the purchase of stocks, plus the costs of bringing them to their existing condition and location, including production OVERHEADS. For most stocks it is either impossible or impracticable to know the precise units of raw materials, and so on, that are being used up in production or that remain at the year end. Thus it is normal for accountants to make assumptions about the flow of such stocks. These include FIRST IN, FIRST OUT (FIFO); LAST IN, FIRST OUT (LIFO); and AVERAGE COST (AVCO). In the UK FIFO and AVCO are normal, whereas LIFO is not allowed for taxation purposes and is discouraged by the relevant ACCOUNTING STANDARDS (SSAP 9). In the United States LIFO is allowed for tax purposes. It is popular there because it usually reduces INCOME.

STRAIGHT-LINE DEPRECIATION

A system of calculating the annual DEPRECIATION expense of FIXED ASSETS. This method charges equal annual instalments against PROFIT over the useful life of the asset. In total, the COST of the asset less any estimated residual value is depreciated. Straight-line depreciation is simple to use and thus very popular.

SUBSIDIARY

Generally an undertaking controlled by another (the parent company).

SUBSTANCE OVER FORM

The presentation in financial statements of the real economic substance of a particular transaction rather than its legal or technical form. (For an example, see LEASE.)

TABLE A

A model set of ARTICLES OF ASSOCIATION to be found in the UK Companies Act. The articles of a COMPANY are the rules that govern the relationships among shareholders, and between shareholders and the company and its directors. A company in the process of formation may adopt or amend Table A for its own purposes.

T-ACCOUNT

See ACCOUNTS.

TANGIBLE ASSETS

ASSETS with a physical existence, such as property, plant or equipment. Tangible assets may be contrasted with investments and with INTANGIBLE ASSETS, such as patents, licences, trade marks or GOODWILL.

TAXABLE INCOME

Annual business net INCOME, as adjusted from accounting rules to tax rules. In the UK there are numerous adjustments from accounting NET PROFIT to taxable income. For example, accounting DEPRECIATION is added back, and CAPITAL ALLOWANCES are granted instead. Dividend income from other companies is deducted, but certain legal fees and entertainment EXPENSES are added back.

TEMPORAL METHOD

The principal method of FOREIGN CURRENCY TRANSLATION used in the United States between 1975 and 1981. It is now only to be used in the US for foreign subsidiaries that are closely integrated with the parent or are in highly inflationary countries. Some German multinational companies also use this method.

TEMPORARY DIFFERENCES

Reversing differences between the tax basis of an asset or liability and its accounting CARRYING VALUE. In the United States ACCOUNTING STANDARDS now require deferred tax to be accounted for on these temporary differences. Many other countries still base deferred taxation on TIMING DIFFERENCES.

TIMES COVERED

Times covered and times interest earned are RATIOS that measure the security of a COMPANY's future DIVIDENDS, INTEREST payments or profits. The times covered or dividend cover normally refers to the number of times that the company's most recent total annual dividends could have been paid out of its annual EARNINGS available for that purpose.

The times interest earned ratio compares the most recent annual interest payments of a company with its NET PROFIT before interest and tax, which is available for such interest payments.

TIMES INTEREST EARNED

See TIMES COVERED.

TIMING DIFFERENCES

Differences, in any period, between TAXABLE INCOME and accounting income which will reverse in a future period. For example, CAPITAL ALLOWANCES often enable plant and machinery to be charged for tax purposes over a shorter period than that used for DEPRECIATION in financial statements. In this case, although the total expense for tax and accounting purposes will eventually be the same, there will be originating and then reversing timing differences. Such timing differences may lead to the need to account for DEFERRED TAX.

TRADE CREDITORS

Suppliers of goods or services to the business who are not paid immediately at the time of purchase. At a BALANCE SHEET date, outstanding amounts owed to them will be shown as trade CREDITORS as part of CURRENT LIABILITIES.

TRADE DEBTORS

Buyers of a business's goods and services who do not pay immediately at the time of purchase. At a BALANCE SHEET date, outstanding amounts owed by them will be shown as trade DEBTORS as part of CURRENT ASSETS.

TRADE MARK

A name or design that a business has a right to use in connection with its products. Accountants will put a value on this for BALANCE SHEET purposes only if that value can be verified because the trade mark was bought or was created using separately identifiable EXPENSES. Thus the value of a trade mark will be recorded as its COST. Trade marks are examples of INTANGIBLE ASSETS.

TRANSFER PRICING

The notional or real price charged by one part of a COMPANY (or group of companies) to another part when goods or services are transferred.

TREASURY STOCK

The US expression for a COMPANY'S SHARES that have been bought back by the company and not cancelled. The shares are held "in the corporate treasury". They receive no DIVIDENDS and carry no votes at company meetings. The UK equivalent term is OWN SHARES. The term treasury stock is confusing to UK readers because it might appear to refer to government bonds.

TRIAL BALANCE

Part of the exercise of producing financial statements from the records in a DOUBLE ENTRY book-keeping system. The trial balance marshals all the DEBIT and CREDIT balances on the various ACCOUNTS on to one page.

TRUE AND FAIR VIEW

The overriding legal requirement for the presentation of financial statements of companies in the UK, the rest of the EU and most of the Commonwealth. It is difficult to tie down an exact meaning to the expression, and it would ultimately have to be interpreted in a court of law. However, the law demands "a" true and fair view, rather than "the" true and fair view; and it is clear that the instruction has to be interpreted in the context of normal accounting practice at the time of the financial statements.

In the UK the law requires that extra information must be disclosed if this is necessary to give a true and fair view. In extreme cases detailed provisions of the law must be departed from if this is the only way of giving a true and fair view. In such cases there must be disclosure of the reasons for and the effects of the departures.

> *We like to feel that, not only do the figures in the balance sheet show you the true position, but that the real position is a little better still.*
> W.E. Hubbard, speech to shareholders at the annual meeting, London and County Bank, *The Economist*, February 7th 1901, p. 204

TURNOVER
The UK expression used in the PROFIT AND LOSS ACCOUNT for the SALES revenue of an accounting period. This is shown net of value added tax.

UITF

See URGENT ISSUES TASK FORCE.

Ultra vires

A Latin expression meaning "beyond the powers". An action of a COMPANY or a director is *ultra vires* if it is beyond the legal powers of the company (as set out in the MEMORANDUM OF ASSOCIATION) or of the director (as set out in the ARTICLES OF ASSOCIATION or in Companies Acts). Such actions may, for example, lead to contracts being void.

UNDERWRITING EXPENSES

The costs incurred when a COMPANY engages a financial institution to underwrite a new issue of SHARES.

UNDISTRIBUTABLE RESERVES

Amounts, paid in by shareholders or notionally allocated out of profits, that are not available for distribution to the shareholders as DIVIDENDS. The US term is RESTRICTED SURPLUS. Undistributable reserves would include SHARE PREMIUM and RESERVES on the REVALUATION OF ASSETS.

UNIFORMITY

The use of the same rules of accounting or financial statement presentation from one COMPANY to another. Improvements in uniformity are encouraged by the setting of ACCOUNTING STANDARDS. One reason for this is to improve comparability between the financial statements of different companies. The word "CONSISTENCY" is often used to mean the use by any individual company of the same accounting methods year by year. This is required by COMPANY LAW.

UNIT TRUSTS

Financial institutions whose main aim is to use the money provided by their investors in order to own and manage profitably a portfolio of investments in other STOCKS and SHARES. Unlike INVESTMENT TRUSTS, they are "open-ended funds" in that their investors will be constantly contributing and withdrawing cash by buying and selling units in the trust. The equivalent US term is MUTUAL FUNDS.

UNLIMITED COMPANY

A legal entity, in the form of a COMPANY, whose shareholders do not have limited liability for the debts of the company. Such companies are fairly rare, but they do have the advantage that some provisions of COMPANY LAW do not apply, including the requirement to publish financial statements.

URGENT ISSUES TASK FORCE

A committee which is part of the standard-setting machinery introduced in the UK in 1990. The Urgent Issues Task Force (UITF) seeks consensus on detailed areas of accounting issues which are already covered by law or by ACCOUNTING STANDARDS. Abstracts of the agreements are then published, and enterprises are expected to obey them so that accounts give a TRUE AND FAIR VIEW.

VALUE ADDED STATEMENTS

Supplementary financial statements prepared by a few companies. They rearrange, and may add to, the information provided in a PROFIT AND LOSS ACCOUNT. The statement begins with a calculation of a measure of total output: SALES, additions to STOCKS (INVENTORIES), other income and FIXED ASSETS created by the business for its own use. Then the statements show deductions from this: amounts paid to suppliers of goods and services, amounts paid to employees, DEPRECIATION, INTEREST, taxation and DIVIDENDS.

VALUE FOR MONEY AUDIT

An investigation of the efficiency of use of resources by organisations whose main aim is not PROFIT. The accountability of some of these bodies is poor. They may have no owners, multiple objectives and no clear measure of success.

VALUE TO THE BUSINESS

See DEPRIVAL VALUE.

VARIABLE COSTS

Costs that vary in proportion to the volume of production. Normally, raw materials and direct labour input will be variable costs. Some overhead costs, which cannot be directly ascribed to particular units of production or processes, may nevertheless still be variable with total production. Variable costs are sometimes called MARGINAL COSTS by accountants. The opposite of these are FIXED COSTS, which do not vary in the short term over the range of production levels being considered.

VARIANCES

Differences between actual amounts of costs, REVENUES, production levels, and so on, and the plans for these amounts set down in a BUDGET.

WEIGHTED AVERAGE COST

A method of determining the COST of STOCKS (INVENTORIES) that are on hand at the end of an accounting period. If a business buys and uses many types of raw materials it might be hard to tell which units have been used and which remain, and thus difficult to calculate the exact costs. It is normal in this case to make flow assumptions such as FIRST IN, FIRST OUT or LAST IN, FIRST OUT or AVERAGE COST. Weighted average cost values units used and units remaining at the average cost of the purchases, weighted by volume. The average may be worked out each time there is another purchase, or at predetermined intervals.

WDV

See WRITTEN DOWN VALUE.

WINDING-UP

The legal procedures for the termination of a COMPANY.

WINDOW DRESSING

The manipulation of figures in financial statements in order to make them appear better (or perhaps worse) than they otherwise would be. (See also CREATIVE ACCOUNTING.)

The accounts are a snapshot of a business at a moment in time. Take a picture the following day and the scene may look very different. As with many of us, companies like to look their best when they are photographed and sometimes dress for the occasion.

M.A. Pitcher, *Management Accounting for the Lending Banker*, 1979, pp. 13–14

WORKING CAPITAL

The difference between CURRENT ASSETS and CURRENT LIABILITIES. This is also known as NET CURRENT ASSETS.

WORK-IN-PROGRESS

Partially manufactured goods on their way from being raw materials to being finished products. Such goods are included in STOCKS (INVENTORIES) and are usually valued at the various costs involved in their production.

WRITING-DOWN ALLOWANCES

Annual DEPRECIATION of FIXED ASSETS for tax purposes in the UK. The allowances form part of the CAPITAL ALLOWANCES system.

WRITTEN DOWN VALUE

The amount at which ASSETS are usually held in BOOKS of account and in financial statements. The written down value (WDV) is the historical cost less an allowance for wearing out, called ACCUMULATED DEPRECIATION. (NET BOOK VALUE has the same meaning.) The same expression may also be used for the amount of an asset that has not yet been allowed as DEPRECIATION for tax purposes; this would be the tax written down value.

YIELD

The earnings yield or the dividend yield of ORDI-NARY SHARES is the latest annual EARNINGS or DIVI-DENDS as a proportion of the market price of the SHARES.

ZBB

See ZERO BASE BUDGETING.

ZERO BASE BUDGETING

A system of budgeting originally developed in the United States for enterprises facing rapid changes in technology and SALES. Zero base budgeting (ZBB) involves a more radical starting from scratch each year than the traditional BUDGET system. Managers must justify their activities as though they were starting for the first time.

Z-SCORE

A measure of the likelihood of a business becoming insolvent. It uses a combination of commonly used RATIOS. The combination has been calculated by studying the ratios of businesses that have failed in the past.

The current fashion for vigorous quantitative analysis has thrown out the baby of relevance in the search for an unimpeachably hygienic variety of methodological bathwater.

A. McCosh and S. Howell

in D. Cooper, R. Scapens and J. Arnold (eds),

Management Accountancy Research and Practice, 1983

---

1 Abbreviations

Here are some of the abbreviations commonly used by accountants. In many cases there are entries for them in the A–Z under the unabbreviated expression.

AAA	American Accounting Association
AARB	Australian Accounting Standards Board
ACA	Associate of the Institute of Chartered Accountants in England and Wales
ACCA	Association of Chartered Certified Accountants, or an Associate of that body
ACMA	Associate of the Chartered Institute of Management Accountants
ACT	advance corporation tax (UK)
AG	*Aktiengesellschaft* (German or Swiss public company)
AGM	annual general meeting
AICPA	American Institute of Certified Public Accountants
AISG	Accountants International Study Group
APB	Accounting Principles Board (USA)
APB	Auditing Practices Board (UK)
APC	Auditing Practices Committee (UK)
ARB	Accounting Research Bulletin
ARS	Accounting Research Study
ASB	Accounting Standards Board (UK)
ASC	Accounting Standards Committee (UK)
ASR	Accounting Series Release of the SEC
BV	*besloten vennootschap* (Dutch or Belgian private company)
CA	chartered accountant
CAPM	capital asset pricing model
CCA	current cost accounting
CCAB	Consultative Committee of Accountancy Bodies (UK and Ireland)
CGT	capital gains tax
CICA	Canadian Institute of Chartered Accountants
CIMA	Chartered Institute of Management Accountants

CIPFA	Chartered Institute of Public Finance and Accountancy
CNC	*Conseil National de la Comptabilité*
CNCC	*Compagnie Nationale des Commissaires aux Comptes*
COB	*Commission des Opérations de Bourse* (Stock Exchange Commission, France)
CONSOB	*Commissione Nazionale per le Società e la Borsa* (Stock Exchange Commission, Italy)
COSA	cost of sales adjustment
CPA	certified public accountant
CPP	current purchasing power accounting
CRC	current replacement cost
cr	credit (in double entry book-keeping)
CVP	cost-volume-profit analysis
DCF	discounted cash flow
dr	debit (in double entry book-keeping)
EAA	European Economic Area
EBIT	earnings before interest and tax
ECU	European currency unit
EDP	electronic data processing
EC	European Community
EFT	electronic funds transfer
EFTPOS	electronic funds transfer at the point of sale
EOQ	economic order quantity
EPS	earnings per share
EU	European Union
EV	economic value
FASB	Financial Accounting Standards Board (USA)
FCA	Fellow of the Institute of Chartered Accountants in England and Wales
FCCA	Fellow of the Association of Chartered Certified Accountants
FCMA	Fellow of the Chartered Institute of Management Accountants
FEE	*Fédération des Experts Comptables Européens*
FIFO	first in, first out
FII	franked investment income
FRC	Financial Reporting Council (UK)
FRED	Financial Reporting Exposure Draft (UK)

FRS	Financial Reporting Standard (UK)
GAAP	generally accepted accounting principles
GAAS	generally accepted auditing standards
GAS	Government Accounting Service (UK)
GASB	Governmental Accounting Standards Board (USA)
GmbH	*Gesellschaft mit beschränkter Haftung* (German or Swiss private company)
IASC	International Accounting Standards Committee
ICAEW	Institute of Chartered Accountants in England and Wales
ICAI	Institute of Chartered Accountants in Ireland
ICAS	Institute of Chartered Accountants of Scotland
IdW	*Institut der Wirtschaftsprüfer*
IFAC	International Federation of Accountants
IOSCO	International Organization of Securities Commissions
IRR	internal rate of return
IRS	International Revenue Service (USA)
JICPA	Japanese Institute of Certified Public Accountants
LIFO	last in, first out
Ltd	Limited (private limited company)
MCT	mainstream corporation tax
MWCA	monetary working capital adjustment
NIVRA	*Nederlands Instituut van Registeraccountants*
NPV	net present value
NRV	net realisable value
NV	*naamloze vennootschap* (Dutch or Belgian public company)
OEC	*Ordre des Experts Comptables*
P/E	price/earnings ratio
P & L a/c	profit and loss account
PLC or plc	public limited company (UK and Ireland)
PRT	petroleum revenue tax (UK)
R&D	research and development
ROCE	return on capital employed

ROI	return on investment
RRA	reserve recognition accounting (for oil and gas)
SA	*société anonyme* (French, Belgian, Luxembourg or Swiss public company)
SARL	*société à responsabilité limitée* (French, etc private company)
SpA	*società per azioni* (Italian public company)
SEC	Securities and Exchange Commission (USA)
SFAC	Statement of Financial Accounting Concepts (USA)
SFAS	Statement of Financial Accounting Standards (USA)
SIB	Securities and Investments Board (UK)
SIC	Standing Interpretations Committee (of the IASC)
SORP	Statement of Recommended Practice (UK)
SSAP	Statement of Standard Accounting Practice (UK)
TB	trial balance
UEC	*Union Européenne des Experts Comptables Economiques et Financiers*
UITF	Urgent Issues Task Force (UK)
USM	Unlisted Securities Market (UK)
VAT	value added tax
VFM	value for money
WDV	written down value
ZBB	zero base budgeting

2 World's largest accountancy firms, 1997

		World fee income $m	UK fee income £m	UK rank
1	Andersen Worldwide	11,300	695	2
2	Ernst & Young	9,100	525	4
3	KPMG	9,000	575	3
4	Coopers & Lybrand	7,541	766	1
5	Deloitte Touche Tohmatsu	7,400	441	6
6	Price Waterhouse	5,620	520	5
7	BDO	1,450	106	8
8	Grant Thornton	1,403	120	7
9	Moores Rowland	1,063	...	...
10	RSM (Robson Rhodes)	1,060	42	10

Note: Coopers & Lybrand and Price Waterhouse have since merged (see pages 55–6).
Source: Adapted from *International Accounting Bulletin*, December 1st 1997 and December 19th 1997.

3 UK accounting standards, 1998

Statements of Standard Accounting Practice (SSAP)

2 Disclosure of accounting policies
3 Earnings per share
4 Government grants
5 Value added tax
8 Taxation
9 Stocks and work in progress
12 Depreciation
13 Research and development
15 Deferred taxation
17 Post balance sheet events
18 Contingencies
19 Investment properties
20 Foreign currency translation
21 Leases and hire purchase
24 Pension costs
25 Segmental reporting

Financial Reporting Standards (FRS)

1 Cash flow accounting
2 Accounting for subsidiary undertakings
3 Reporting financial performance
4 Capital instruments
5 Substance of transactions
6 Acquisitions and mergers
7 Fair values in acquisition accounting
8 Related party transactions
9 Associates and joint ventures
10 Goodwill and intangible assets

4 Useful addresses

Institute of Chartered Accountants in England and Wales
Chartered Accountants' Hall
Moorgate Place
London EC2P 2BJ
Telephone: +44 171 920 8100

Association of Chartered Certified Accountants
29 Lincoln's Inn Fields
London WC2A 3EE
Telephone: +44 171 242 6855

Chartered Institute of Management Accountants
63 Portland Place
London W1N 4AB
Telephone: +44 171 637 2311

Institute of Chartered Accountants of Scotland
27 Queen Street
Edinburgh EH2 1LA
Telephone: +44 131 225 5673

Chartered Institute of Public Finance and Accountancy
2 Robert Street
London WC2N 6BH
Telephone: +44 171 930 3456

Institute of Chartered Accountants in Ireland
87 Pembroke Road
Dublin 4
Telephone: +353 1 680400

Institute of Chartered Accountants in Ireland
11 Donegal Square South
Belfast BT1 5JE
Telephone: +44 1232 21600

INTERNATIONAL

Fédération des Experts Comptables Européens
Rue de la Loi 83
1040 Bruxelles
Belgium
Telephone: +32 2 285 4085

International Accounting Standards Committee
166 Fleet Street
London EC4A 2DY
UK
Telephone: +44 171 353 0565

International Federation of Accountants
114 West 47th Street
Suite 2410
New York
NY 10036
USA
Telephone: +1 212 302 5952

5 Recommended reading

THE AUTHOR

General
Christopher Nobes, *Introduction to Financial Accounting*, Routledge, London, 1997.

Taxation
Simon James and Christopher Nobes, *The Economics of Taxation*, Prentice-Hall, Hemel Hempstead, 1997/98.

Comparisons with other countries
Christopher Nobes, *International Guide to Interpreting Company Accounts,* Financial Times Reports, 1996.

C.W. Nobes and R.H. Parker, *Comparative International Accounting*, Prentice-Hall, Hemel Hempstead, 1998.

OTHER AUTHORS

Cooper & Lybrand, *Manual of Accounting,* Accountancy Books, 1998.

Ernst & Young, *UK GAAP*, Macmillan, London, latest edition.

Ernst & Young, *UK/US GAAP Comparison* (3rd edition), Kogan Page, London, 1994.

R.H. Parker, *Macmillan Dictionary of Accounting* (2nd edition), Macmillan, London, 1992.